Magpie Boy

Also by Beth Roberts
The little Lake Who Cried
(*five editions 1976–1988*)
Manganinnie 1979
reprinted 1980
French edition 1984
Japanese edition 1988
New English edition 1988
The Upside-Down Bird 1987
The Wombat Who Couldn't See in the Dark 1987
The Tasmanian Devil Who Couldn't Eat Meat 1988

Arts for
Australians
Australia **Council**

This publication assisted by the Australia Council, the Australian
Government's arts funding and advisory body.

Magpie Boy

by
Beth Roberts

For the Gillemore Library
Lochalsh.
Greetings from
Tasmania

Beth Roberts
1 - 2 - 1992

JBCE

Melbourne

Published by
THE JOINT BOARD OF CHRISTIAN EDUCATION
Second Floor, 10 Queen Street, Melbourne 3000, Australia

National Library of Australia
 Cataloguing-in-Publication entry.

Roberts, Beth.
 Magpie boy.

 ISBN 0 85819 756 1.

 I. Joint Board of Christian Education. II. Title.

A823'.3

First printed 1989

Design: Kelvin Young
Illustrators: cover, G. Cook; section headings, Janet Fenton
Typeset: Bookset Pty Ltd
Printer: The Book Printer

JB/1738

Contents

Part Four

Part Five

Foreword

Beth Roberts in her classic story *Manganinnie* proved that the past is not irretrievably lost. The imagination and sensitivity of an artist in words can recreate times past and people gone, not perhaps exactly as they were but certainly as they might have been. A fiction, skilfully blending elements of fantasy and reality, can penetrate more deeply into the essential truth of people, places and events than can a merely factual telling.

In *Magpie Boy*, Beth Roberts returns to the land and life of the Tasmanian Aborigines in the early years of European settlement. With so much of Aboriginal culture in the island unrecorded and unremembered, she enriches us by her imaginative recreation of how their life, their relationships, their perceptions and their struggles might have been.

In and through her central character, Dreenee, we become aware how, in the encounter between two very different races, the consciousness and sensibility of each is profoundly affected. This powerful book gives a personal and human dimension to the cold phrase "clash of cultures". There is a tragic irony in Beth Roberts' plot as she reveals the potential for relationship between white and black in that brief space of years when tragedy had not yet become inevitable.

Each of us, I think, hears "magpie voices" in our life, sometimes to guide, sometimes to chide. We find some symbol, some metaphor, some source of inspiration to help us make sense of the strange, to find courage in the face of the alarming, and to give us direction in an uncharted future. Thus, Dreenee and his magpies are not merely part of a lovingly-crafted and localised myth but contribute to the important literature of the general human condition.

Glenn C Pullen
Supervisor of Libraries
Education Department of Tasmania

7

A note from the author

The factual information in this story comes chiefly from the Journal kept by George Augustus Robinson, made available through the monumental work of Tasmania's classic historian N.J.B. Plomley. *Friendly Mission, The Tasmanian Journals* and *Papers of George Augustus Robinson, 1829–1834*, edited by N.J.B. Plomley, was published by the Tasmanian Historical Research Association in 1966.

I am extremely privileged to have had Brian Plomley provide me with relevant material, and tutor me with steadfast precision and tolerance during the writing of *Manganinnie*. Furthermore he kindly recommended me for a grant, and has given generously of his time with this work, for all of which I thank him deeply. I am also grateful to him for sharing with me the following quotation, which makes my central character's conversations with the magpies, for many of us, more wholly believable, and gives us further insight into the unique affinity of the tribal Aborigines with the creatures of their Motherland:

"After supper we had an opportunity of observing one of the superstitions of the Aboriginal natives, an owl, one of the species called by the colonists More Pork having perched upon a tree near to our break wind began to hoot his evening note. The two blacks attached to the party started up and began an earnest conversation principally addressed to the bird who occasionally hooted his responses on hearing which they shouted with the most extravagant demonstrations of joy. When this whimsical conversation ceased Tom explained to us that the bird (which he called COCOLO DIANA) was capable of giving any information he required concerning his wandering countrymen. Tom interpreted to us the conversation by which we had just been amused but as we did not place much faith in Mr Cocolo's information it is not worth recording what his votaries informed us he had communicated to them." (Extract from a report by Gilbert Robertson, 1829, in Colonial Secretary's archives, State Library of Tasmania.)

For the Literary Fellowship awarded to me by the Aboriginal Board of the Australia Council, I wish to express my appreciation; also to the numerous persons who have nurtured me in the evolution of my story, including Peter Murray, Glenn Pullen, Mary McRae, Helgar Walker, Robyn Friend and Janet Fenton. I also thank the Tasmanian Environment Centre for the word-processing of my manuscript, and all typists and readers.

Finally, I whole-heartedly thank Helen Gee for her hard work, enthusiasm and innate sensitivity as editor.

Beth Roberts.

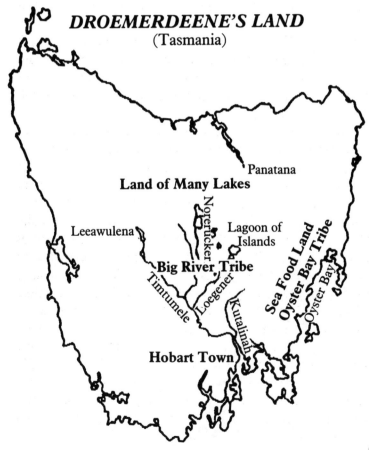

DROEMERDEENE'S LAND
(Tasmania)

Panatana

Land of Many Lakes

Leeawulena

Norerucker

Lagoon of Islands

Big River Tribe

Sea Food Land

Oyster Bay Tribe

Oyster Bay

Tirntumele

Loegener

Kutalinah

Hobart Town

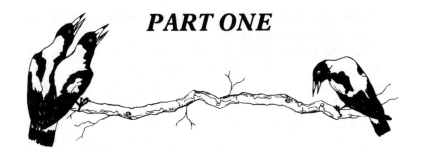

PART ONE

1. Raindrops

All night long wind howled, calling rain. Lightning flashed and thunder rumbled and then, just before dawn, rain fell in cold relentless sweeps. Rain, washing the land clean of summer dusts, tearing away dead twigs and bark; rain carrying brittle waiting seeds high in the dark night air.

Around the campfire the Big River People slept close together; all except Moonah. She waited, wide-eyed and restless, listening to the fury of the night, waiting for her time to move away from her People.

Firelight cast long flickering shadows on the walls of the cave and Moonah let her thoughts flicker with them across the sleeping forms of her People.

Now and then lightning flashed and for that moment the sleeping place was flooded with light, brighter than sunlight, shadowless, and she could see everyone clearly. Only an arm's length away, Leenameena, her husband, stirred and slept fitfully, hugging to his chest the thick warm skin of a kangaroo. Fondly watching him Moonah thought about the old legend of how the Ancestral Beings sent children in raindrops. Soon she would be mother and he would be father; for at last the rain had come. Not just gentle raindrops, but drenching rain. Knowing this new one who was coming through her would be strong and fearless, Moonah smiled, feeling the strength of the child's coming and then she quietly moved away to find a place where the grasses were sweet and green.

Wind and rain pounded her strong young body as she struggled towards the creek.

Carrying only a firestick and a large kangaroo skin, she followed the well-worn track of the bush creatures. Trees moaned and creaked, bending to the will of the wind while Moonah bent to the will of the new life within her. Pausing and moving on, she wended her way through the sedges and bracken until she reached a huge spreading candlebark beside the creek. Here she sheltered, cumbersome and short of breath, half leaning against the strong trunk and comforted by the strength of the old tree; glad to be out of the wind; glad of the wet refreshing rain.

Moonah busied herself collecting dry bark and twigs from a hollow bole of the tree. Very soon she was ready, squatting down over fresh leaves, close to her little fire.

Rain thrashed relentlessly at the gumtree, but it had known many storms. With widespread limbs it kept the waiting place dry. Runnels of water collected in the boles and overflowed. Tapered leaves bent earthward with the weight of the water, but the little fire crackled merrily, where no raindrops could reach it. Moonah had chosen her waiting place well. Fire glowed, crowding out the darkness and the spirits who dwelt in the dark places.

Waiting . . . listening to the rushing creek nearby, Moonah felt the powerful thrust of the life-force which was now beyond her will. Breathing deeply she waited for the next wave, each wave coming closer together and stronger, part of her, yet like the waters of the swollen creek, not belonging to her, as the waters did not belong to the creek.

Beyond the darkness she could feel the nearness of the Old Ones watching over her from their campfires in the River of Stars. Even though they were hidden by rain, it was a comfort to know they were there. Beyond the fire she could see no stars; only the windswept rain; only the raindrops gathering on and clinging to the leaves of her candlebark tree. Watching them fall all around her, Moonah felt the head of the new life leave her body. Then, quite suddenly, the child came. And just as suddenly the winds stood still and the rain stopped and nearby the song of the first magpie echoed in the peaceful gully.

A warm glow washed over the young mother, taking away the memory of the long lone night. She focused her whole being on this new boy-child.

How strongly did he cry, and then draw from her milk!

Contentedly Moonah cradled her first-born child in her arms, breathing in the familiar smell of the sweet wet earth; breathing in the sweet new smell of her son.

Listening to the steady rhythm of his breathing and the melodious morning song of the magpies, Moonah felt drowsy. Soon the two sounds fused together and drifted with her into a deep refreshing sleep.

2. Guardians

Dawn came softly after the rain. Pale shafts of sunlight slid across the fresh-washed Land. Then slowly the colours swelled, and a brilliant orange light painted the sunburnt grasses and, moving down into the gully, reached the huge candlebark tree and shone on the tiny face of Moonah's newborn child. He turned his face towards the new warmth.

Other movement, not part of his own being, surrounded him. Things moving and making noises. Sound was also new. The little one soaked up the new sounds. A flock of magpies was strutting forward on the sunlit grass and making a black and white circle around him. Unaware, the new man-child stretched his legs enjoying his own movement, and the sounds around him. The magpies warbled softly. They scratched about in the sweet wet earth while each bird gave the child a now-and-then sideways look.

The magpies took one long look at the tiny person, feeling compassion for him, knowing that one day he would have the gift of vision like his noble grandfather, and that from this day forward they would become his guardians.

13

They then flew up into the sunlit branches of a nearby tree where they sang their beautiful sunrise song.

Ningermaner woke with a start. Her shoulder was twitching urgently, telling her someone needed her. Instantly wide awake, she looked to the place where Moonah usually slept and, finding it empty, smiled to herself.

Quickly she collected a kangaroo skin and kindled a firestick from the campfire. Then she stole away to follow her daughter. Her gentle eyes glowed with excitement as she hurried along as fast as her old legs would carry her.

A flock of magpies circled down the gully as she approached the creek. There, under the ancient candlebark tree, she found her daughter sleeping peacefully in a shaft of sunlight, and in her arms a small brown bundle of boy. Two strong little arms were stretched above his head, and his face was turned towards the rays of the sun.

Ningermaner was beside herself with joy. How big and strong he looked!

It was good to be a grandmother once more. A tear rolled down her wrinkled cheek, leaving a crooked runnel in the animal fat smeared on her face, and an aching chord caught in the back of her throat where the Song of the People trembled. Three soft clear notes flowed out over the Land, repeated again and again. She slipped noiselessly away to find food. Moonah would be hungry when she woke.

Many small creatures always came to the creek to drink when Sun first shone on the Land. Beyond the creek a rat kangaroo was gathering the native bread from the underside of a fallen tree. Close by him two echidnas waddled about feeding on ants and termites in the rotten wood, their long sticky tongues flicking out and curling around their early morning meal.

Ningermaner was about to paddle across the creek and stalk an echidna when a blue-tongued lizard slid through the bushes right beside her, and settled to sun himself on a flat rock. She stood motionless watching him, and while she waited his eyes became mere slits and his fat young body so still he was hard to see.

In a flash Ningermaner killed him and soon had him cooking on the hot coals.

Sitting close to the fire the old woman watched and waited to hear her grandson cry for his mother's milk; waited to fuss over her daughter.

Smoke curled in a brilliant sky, and the smell of food wafted in a gentle breeze. Seeds and twigs swept past her, swirling away on the top of the swollen creek and the sky was busy with birds.

A kingfisher glided past Ningermaner flying low, fishing the creek for the little mountain trout. Now and then scarlet robins and blue wrens flitted from twig to twig, and high in the trees the magpies were singing more sweetly than she had ever heard them. Perhaps they were happy to see another new baby; or perhaps it was for the grasshoppers which were hatching after the wonderful rain? Ningermaner wasn't sure. Certainly there were plenty of magpies about today. Even as she waited for Moonah to stir, another colony of them arrived and circled overhead.

From the very first day, Ningermaner adored her grandson. He was the image of her husband and the idol of her eyes. Even Warrabee could feel a strong attraction to his new grandson though the child was only one of three new babes belonging to his daughters and daughter-in-law. He had quietly observed that Moonah's baby was always the first in the camp to wake and he was always hungry. Even after Moonah had fed him, and his stomach was tight and round like a frog's, he didn't doze contentedly like Manganinnie's and Nunnelarie's babies. Instead he would kick and yell, wanting to roll out from under his warm possum skin. He had a very loud cry.

Every day Ningermaner looked forward to her time with Moonah's little boy-child. While Manganinnie's and Nunnelarie's babies were only interested in looking at their own hands, and learning to smile and focus their eyes, this one was reaching out and taking leaves and flowers and feathers. He would even turn them over and taste them, or transfer them from one hand to the other.

Many small birds lived in the gully, and sometimes the old woman would imitate the high-pitched reel of the blue wren as it flitted from twig to twig, or the deeper chattering trill of the scarlet robin. The little one was always fascinated, and he soon learnt that if he kept very still the tiny birds would hop closer. Keeping still was the very first lesson about stalking and hunting, so Ningermaner was happy. She loved teaching the little children all about the creatures of the bush and she loved imitating bird calls. All her life she had collected bird calls like bees collect honey, so she had much Common Knowledge about them to share.

One morning when Moonah's child was just learning to sit up alone, and the other two summer babies were still only able to roll about, he uttered his first three peals of magpie song.

Everyone was amazed. Even his grandfather, Warrabee, who was Leader of all the Big River people, heard the news and came to listen.

"He's a real little magpie", Ningermaner said to her husband that night when they were alone around their own fire, "and growing so fast! Did you know he can almost crawl?"

Warrabee chuckled affectionately, and warned his wife not to have favourites. It was her place to help with all the little children; but nevertheless, when Warrabee returned from hunting next day, he had a half-grown wombat tucked in a possum skin and quite unashamedly he gave it to Moonah's baby!

Watching the women and children crowd round the fat furry creature, Ningermaner said nothing, but she couldn't help chuckling to herself. Her grandson was the centre of attention. He sat nursing the young wombat which was almost his own size, while Warrabee squatted down beside him. When the wombat wriggled away, all the children formed a circle around it, making a coughing noise just like the young creature.

The boy kicked and yelled, wanting to hold the furry creature again, but no-one took any notice; not until

Warrabee got down on his hands and knees beside him and began crawling towards the wombat. Soon all the children were crawling and rolling about, laughing. Only Moonah's baby sat silently thinking. Yelling and kicking did no good. Perhaps he too could crawl like the bigger boys? Watching him, his mother came to the rescue. She put him in the crawling position and began rocking his little body backwards and forwards. Copying the others, he crawled forward one arm's length; then he toppled over, smiling broadly!

Moments later one of the children put the wombat back in his arms, while Leenameena came forward with a hollow log and showed his son how wombats like to hide away from the bright sunlight. The wombat shuffled his head and shoulders into the dark place and the little boy sat contentedly fondling the rump of the creature, well pleased with himself.

3. The Three Summer Babies

One starlight night when Moon was full, the three summer babies were given names.

As was the custom, the name was chosen to suit the personality of the child, or the time and place of the birth, so when Warrabee called for Manganinnie and Meenapeek-ameena to bring their fourth-born child forward, they proudly gave the name of "Lugga" (which means foot-prints, or tracks) because he always seemed to be playing with his feet; and the old Chief rubbed red ochre into the soles of the small one's feet.

"Greetings, Lugga", he said.

"May you travel safely and well all the days of your life and learn to understand many tracks."

Little Lugga seemed well pleased with his name, for he smiled contentedly, kicking his legs when he was handed back to his parents.

Next, Moonah and Leenameena were called to come

forward with their first-born child. It was a happy moment for the young couple as they gave the name Dreenee (which means magpie), for it was obvious to them that their child was much attracted to the magpies and, like the magpies, was very clever.

"Greetings, Dreenee", Warrabee said.

"May you be as clever as a magpie from this day forward, and learn from the magpies. They are your friends, and one day you will be their messenger."

With great care Warrabee rubbed the centre of Dreenee's broad brow with the red ochre, and the little boy's eyes never left the face of his grandfather; nor did they smile. For one fleeting moment Warrabee saw the red eyes of a magpie shining inside Dreenee's own big brown ones; then he handed him back to Moonah and called next for his daughter Nunnelarie and her husband Leewan to come to him with their girl-child, whose name they gave as Puggalena (which means sunrise). Warrabee gazed long and well at the dainty little Puggalena, feeling her gentle ways. He felt strong and protective as he cradled her in his arms. She was indeed soft as a summer sunrise.

Tenderly he powdered her cheeks with the sacred red ochre.

"Greetings, Puggalena. May you ever be soft and warm as a summer sunrise, and a great comfort to your family", he said.

After Lugga, Dreenee and little Puggalena were settled down together on a large kangaroo skin close to the warmth of the fire, a special song was sung for each one, followed by a song for the Old Ones who had sent the three summer babies in the raindrops. Then there was much feasting succeeded by more songs and dances. But Ningermaner slipped away to her own private fire after she had eaten. Soon Warrabee would join her; however just for now she wanted to be alone.

It was a beautiful night. Moon was fat and round and in the next gully magpies were warbling softly in the moonlight.

Pensively the old Aborigine blew on the coals of her fire and fed them long dry needles of the she-oak. She had much to think about. Dreenee's eyes worried her. While Lugga and Puggalena had smiled and looked about when their song was sung, Dreenee had a faraway look in his eyes. He simply focused them on the flames in the campfire, seemingly unaware of his parents and friends. Ningermaner was concerned. Later she would talk about it to her husband, but now she wanted time to think.

Her small fire flickered cheerfully as she sat pondering over Dreenee. Fire spirits twinkled and twirled in the flames, then quite suddenly she heard someone calling her name: "Ningermaner". The Voice came from the glowing coals, and Ningermaner recognised it as the voice of her old father. From his campfire in the River of Stars her father was speaking! Ningermaner's whole body trembled with the wonder of his words:

I greet you, my child. I come to speak of the many changes in the Land of Southern Star. The pale-faced people kill the seals on the shores and the whales in the deep waters. They steal our women. Soon many more will come. The Land will see new ways and there will be much sadness and many changes. The People will need a strong leader.

The magpies are Dreenee's guardians. When he is older they will bring news to him. He must listen to them and share what he hears with the Elders, for one day Dreenee will be our leader, and the Old Ones have chosen you to be his childhood teacher.

Teach your little magpie boy to look and listen well and to become cunning and fearless.

After the voice of her father had faded away Ningermaner pensively fed the coals with twigs and looked towards the river of stars above. How bright was every star tonight! How close were the Old Ones! Moon was climbing high, but Ningermaner wasn't sleepy. She began to think carefully about Dreenee. It was almost as if she had always known that he was bigger and stronger than any other child who had known only four full moons. Already he could sit up and roll over, and was just beginning to crawl.

Ningermaner planned the day to come. The older children would practise stone-throwing and reading tracks, and climbing rocks and trees, while the little ones would play looking and listening games. Then she would collect all the children together for a story.

Ningermaner tried to think of all the New Knowledge which had been added to Common Knowledge since she was a child. Nothing had changed in their own tribal land. Only in the Seafood Land had New Knowledge been added. News of the big sailing ships was now Common Knowledge.

More ships than she had fingers had been seen. The first time, the peculiar pale-skinned people had come ashore and collected fresh water and a few pieces of plants, and gone away again without seeing the People. But later another party met the People and gave them necklaces and other trinkets. Mostly they did not see the People hiding and watching them, and they went away again. Their pale skins fascinated and frightened the People. At first they had thought the spirits of their dead ones were returning, but now they knew of course that they were real people with strange ways. Spirit People did not leave tracks behind them. There were stories of every ship sighted; all had been added to Common Knowledge and shared.

Gazing into the fire, Ningermaner could see again her mother's face, and feel the excitement of the story of the first ship as it was told to her in song and dance when she herself was a child. And the story of the pale-skinned man who swam ashore and planted a straight dead tree! Soon everyone had rocked with laughter around the campfire, as one of the young men pretended to swim ashore carrying a dead tree and plant it in the ground. This was the first story about the pale-faced people and a great favourite with the children. Tomorrow she must make sure that all the little children knew it because Ningermaner sensed the beginning of change for the People of Droemerdeene's Land.

4. The Call of the Sea

For one whole cycle of Moon the Land gave them food as the Big River tribe followed their new Chief, Mannerganner, along the ancient pathway to the Sea.

Crossing a river, the Kutalinah, they walked out of their own territory, and then with great respect stayed close to *markomemenyer* the path as they travelled through other tribal territories, for this was the Law. Sometimes they stayed several days at one campsite, and sometimes only overnight. There was no hurry and there was nothing to fear by day and only the Evil Spirits by night. News had been passed on through Common Knowledge about the pale-faced Intruders who now hunted *naweetya* the seal on the rocks, and killed *mitawennya* the whale in the deep waters; but these evil ones belonged to the salt water. There was no record of their walking on the Land. *Naweetya* did not walk on the Land and neither did these pale-faced ones. The people had nothing to fear walking in the Land belonging to the Oyster Bay tribe. The two tribes shared the seasonal foods. When summer came in the Land of Many Lakes the Oyster Bay tribe walked in the Land of the Big River tribe, and shared with them the great Festival of the Eggfood Season.

Sometimes they slept in caves as they travelled through the hills and gullies and when there were no caves they built their bark wind-breaks in a sheltered spot, always close to water. Following the same ancient pathway, they visited the same hunting grounds and ceremonial sites, and always they did their cooking at the same middens. Here the bones of many a feast were piled high. *Trullerner* the wind and *poekenner* the rain had weathered them, making the campsite clean again; and here many stone and bone implements lay about, ready to be used again and left for the next season. Occasionally they hunted in large groups, but usually families formed into small groups, exchanging news and teaching their children the habits of the creatures, for each gully and every creek and lake had its own magic.

Many of the young women carried a baby on their backs, snug in a warm carry skin of the kangaroo. Together with the babies, there were digging sticks and rush baskets and, most important, *poorena* the firestick to be carried by the women. But the men carried only their spears, walking in front of the women, their spears poised and ready to throw, for they were the hunters of the large animals. Even the carrying of *larner* the kangaroo and *gonnanner* the emu they tried to avoid, while the women and the older children were often well laden with food and skins, climbing ropes and baskets made of rushes. These contained stone implements and articles of adornment, such as shell necklaces and pieces of red ochre, which would be needed for the festivals or traded for something else with other tribes. There was often much for them to carry, yet they always had time to play with the children and sing and laugh, for there was never any hurry. At the end of the day there was always more singing and story-telling around *tonna* the campfire.

Fire was very important to them. It cooked their food, gave them light and warmth and burnt their dead and it kept *Raegeowropper* the Evil Spirit of night away. Even the smoke was important, for it kept away the stinging insects and told others of their whereabouts. The ashes were used for mixing with animal fat for smearing over their bodies and also for healing wounds and raising the ceremonial and ornamental scars. The keeping of the firestick was very important, since the People had not been given the knowledge of making fire by friction, so *poorena* was perhaps their most important and most sacred possession.

As the People walked towards the morning sun their mountains grew smaller and paler, and the call of Lynoteyer the Sea grew stronger. Around the campfires at night they practised the ancient songs which belonged to Lynoteyer. Little children were taught the story of *naweetya* the seal, and *marweyanner* the dolphin and *toebenanner* the fairy penguin, and the men moved away from the women to talk about safety. For several winters now there had been a new fear of the pale-faced ones who came over the rim of their

World and sometimes took away the food which belonged to the People. The men talked for a long time about keeping fires small and posting a scout along the headlands to watch for *triggelune*, the sailing ships on the sea, and *lugga* the tracks of the toeless ones on the sand.

For many nights they talked about the strange toeless tracks left on the sand, Common Knowledge now for many cycles of the seasons. Of the Big River tribe, only Mannerganner had actually seen them, so one night he gave to his tribe a new song and dance about the Toeless Ones.

A pale-faced man was swimming in the sea. When he came up out of the water and sat on a rock he had no covering on his pink body, and we definitely saw five toes on the end of each foot! We crept closer along the rocks, until the Intruder was only a stone's throw away and then we flattened ourselves on the big black rock to look and listen. So curious were we that we turned our back on the Sea, forgetting Sea, until suddenly Sea took away the Old Chief.

Mannerganner pondered over this story, for it was the Law not to mention the name of a dead one. For days he had planned his story, careful not to mention the Old Chief by name. Everyone watched him, wide-eyed, and the women and children laughed, wriggling their own brown toes. Only Ningermaner did not laugh. When the song and dance of the Toeless Ones was finished she moved away to sit alone by *tonna* and rock out the sadness which tugged at her heart, heavy and cold as a stone from the river-bed.

5. Magpie Magic

Five times the ancient food-gathering cycle had travelled full circle for Dreenee and he could now run quite fast. He was even learning to swim underwater and he could climb a small tree faster than any boy who had known only five bloomings of *draydee* the wattle. He was big for his age and he knew this. One of his favourite games was to look at his own shadow, but he was always very careful to look at it only when Sun first walked in the Land or just before he slipped away behind the hills, for this was the best time. He even talked to his shadow, telling it to grow fast so that he would be a big strong warrior like his father; and every time he talked to it, somewhere, not far away, the magpies would flutter down and watch him. Sometimes he talked to them, but always they had stared back at him in total silence. It was very confusing for the small boy. Other birds did not stare at him and follow him around. Certainly he loved them more than any other family of birds, but that was only because they had such a beautiful song. Once he had even tried to practise magic on them, so they would go away, but it didn't work. Always they had stared and had followed him wherever the food-gathering pattern called his family.

Today, for the first time, the magpies actually strutted up very close to him and silently stared. What bright blood-red eyes each bird had!

Even as he watched, their eyes grew brighter and brighter and he could almost feel their thoughts flowing into his mind, simply by being close to them.

It was a strange new feeling for the little boy and he was surprised to find he was not afraid. In fact he felt rather important and at the same time, very curious.

"What do you want?" he asked them; but it was no use. They only moved closer and stared so hard that their eyes were now brighter than sunrise.

"Well, if you won't tell me, I'll go and ask Ningermaner. She knows everything," he said, starting to feel rather uncomfortable.

Dreenee began to turn his head and look about for his grandmother, but his head would only turn a little way and his eyes would not look away from the magpies' eyes! He tried to move away but his body stayed in the same place! Meanwhile the magpies began to warble softly, so he decided to close his eyes. But they would not stay shut. Something made him want to look and listen to the magpies and he could do nothing about it. He was under their spell! Dreenee didn't know how long he had been sitting with his eyes fixed on the big birds when suddenly they chortled loudly, startling him and, rising in the air, they flew up into a tree on the other side of the river. Looking about him Dreenee saw Lugga and a noisy crowd of other little friends coming closer and just in front of them a bandicoot darted, zigzagging in and out among the tussocks, squealing in terror.

Moments later Dreenee joined in the chase, yelling loudly with the children as they circled round the tussocks, hurling stones until the little animal was captured and killed.

The excitement was over and Dreenee now had time to think. It had been good to run and yell after such a mysterious experience with the magpies, and he even wondered if perhaps he had been dreaming. He looked across the river and there, high in some yellow gums, he saw the magpies and knew it was no dream.

Quickly he looked away from them before they could put a holding spell on him and he hurried down to conceal himself in a clump of wattles beside the River of Singing Waters.

His little legs were shaking and he needed time to sort through his feelings before he went to look for Ningermaner.

Pensively Dreenee sat listening to the merry music of the river as the waters bubbled and bounced their way over the shiny smooth stones. Presently tiny waterspirits came to twinkle and twirl in the rock pools, and he spoke to them: "I wish you would sit still. I can't think when you are splashing about and having such fun". He was really testing out his powers, and was pleased when they sat down in a little circle; but when they began staring at him he felt uncomfortable. Supposing their magic was as strong as the magpies' and he could not send them away? There was only one way to find out: "Go away, little water spirits. I'm sorry but I want to be alone", he said. In a flash they were gone and Dreenee was glad. He wondered about the tree spirits. Would they come if he called?

"Come here, tree spirits", he said. "I want to talk to you".

Suddenly the trees were crowded.

"Wah! Wah!" he exclaimed. "I can call you up and send you away, but I do wish someone would tell me more about magpie-magic. It is stronger than mine, and I am not sure if I liked being under their spell. I couldn't even look away or walk away when they stared at me just now. What do they want?"

Dreenee was now tired with so much excitement and concentration, so he flattened himself on the grass and closing his eyes, collected his thoughts together.

It was good to know he could call up the tree spirits and the water spirits and send them away and could almost understand their language, but there was nothing unusual about that. All the little children could do this at about the same time as they learned to sing and dance. Lugga was the same age and he played lots of games with them. Even some of the mothers and fathers could still enjoy the company of the spirits who lived in water and fire and trees, but he had never heard of anyone being held under the spell of magpies. Certainly there was a lot of magic in the air today, and tomorrow it would grow stronger, he knew, because Moon had only one more day to grow round and ready for the important Festival of Droemerdeene.

Ningermaner was mixing together some animal fat and ashes when Dreenee found her. As he flung himself down beside her and looked inside her eyes she immediately sensed that her grandson's mind was heavy with confusion, so she gave him her full attention.

"Ningermaner", he asked her, "Why do the magpies stare at me and follow me about?"

Carefully the old woman chose her words before she spoke.

"The magpies are your guardians, little Dreenee", she told him.

"But how do you know they are?" he asked her.

"My help-spirits tell me many things. The magpies have secrets they wish to share with you. When they call you, do not be afraid. Just open your mind to them and close it to everything else, for each time they will have a message which they want you to share with the People when the time is ready."

Ningermaner sat quietly for several moments, rubbing the soothing ashes and fat into her grandson's skin and then she spoke again:

"Do you know of the important part the magpies played in the dark Waiting Time, before the Dreamtime? You have already heard the story around the campfire several times. Can you tell it to me now?"

Dreenee tried very hard to remember it, but all he could think of was magpies with long sticks. So Ningermaner made sure they could not be seen or interrupted, settled herself down, lifted Dreenee on to her knees and began to tell him once again the Dreamtime story:

Long long ago the sky was so close to the earth that the sun was shut out. There was not even room to stand up, so everyone had to crawl about in the darkness feeling for food with their hands, until the magpies had a very clever idea. They decided that if they all worked together they could lift the sky up with long sticks and make more room for everyone to move about.

Together they worked, lifting the sky first on to low boulders and then on to higher boulders, until everyone could stand upright. Then while they were struggling to lift the sky even higher it suddenly split open, and the sun shone on them bringing light and warmth!

The magpies were overjoyed to see the glorious sunrise, and they burst into their sunrise song; and even today at sunrise and sunset they sing to remind us of that important occasion long, long ago.

Dreenee listened in fascination to every word Ningermaner spoke and when she had finished he laughed excitedly.

"Aren't I lucky, Ningermaner!" he exclaimed, "to have the same name as the magpies. I did not like it until now!"

"Yes, my little one, you are truly a magpie boy, so learn all you can about them for you have been chosen as their messenger, just as I have been chosen to be your teacher."

6. Festival of Droemerdeene

Dreenee wandered down to the banks of the River of Singing Waters to practise his magic on the little water spirits who twinkled and twirled in the bubbling flow, or sat in tiny circles on the smooth wet stone. Perhaps if he asked them, they could tell him more about the magpies. *Wetar* the moon had only one day to grow fat and round, ready for the great Festival of Droemerdeene, the Southern Star who made the first black man.

Instead of romping about with the other children Dreenee stayed with his own shadow. He stood up, straight as a little blue-gum sapling, and made a magic circle around himself and his shadow, keeping out other children and keeping in learning and remembering. Crawling into a hollow log just big enough to turn around in, he looked about.

It was a cozy old log, smelling of droppings of *drogermutter* the wombat, and dank crumbling wood where spiders spun their delicate filaments and fat grubs worked tirelessly, churning their way through the decaying wood. From here he could see the smokes of many families as they moved slowly down the tiers from the Land of Many Lakes and over the boulder-strewn plains from Leeawulena, the Lake of Dreams. Beside him tumbled the singing waters and only a stone's throw away he could see his mother laughing and chattering around the fire with other women who had already arrived; and all about the children yelled and frolicked, feeling the excitement of the great festival. Ningermaner he could see disappearing along the path towards a small group walking into camp. Her long legs were covering the ground with leaps of joy and her arms were outstretched to welcome them. Soon he saw her scoop up a new baby from a young woman's arms, and as they moved closer he realised that it was Manganinnie and her family. He wanted to run to greet his aunt and play with his cousins but he pushed the idea out of his head and looked to the place where the men were busy around another small fire, heating their spears in the flames to make them straight and strong. As they worked they chanted a ritual song and the small boy could see with his magic eye the circle of pink light which protected them from being overheard.

All next day more groups arrived on the banks of Norerucker Menanyer and the excitement grew. Tonight *Wetar* would be as round as the tiny balls of yellow blossom, and ready to hear the songs of the People.

Dreenee kept to himself, looking and listening and storing New Knowledge in his mind. Sometimes he watched from his log, and sometimes he climbed up into a wattle tree or a wild cherry tree. Men were bringing food to the fire, ready for the feast which would follow the special songs and dances, and the women hurried about. Bodies were blackened with ashes and fat and tribal markings were traced with white clay and *ballawinne* the sacred red ochre. Feathers and flowers were collected to adorn the hair and shell necklaces were polished until they shone. The women laughed and joked as they shaved each other's hair according to the custom. Men were busy arranging their own hair with great care and pride. Fat and red ochre were rubbed together and then coils of hair were rolled between the hands into thick red ropes.

The world was new and fragrant with the perfumes of flowering trees and shrubs. Nests were being built, some high in the trees and others in stumps and tussocks and in the sandy banks beside the singing waters. The ants were busy unsealing their galleries and in the damp mosses earthworms were stirring again. Everywhere he looked and listened Dreenee found something exciting happening.

29

Heath and flag lilies covered the slopes and in the shady places tiny violets and buttercups smiled up at him. Cicadas were singing as they sucked up the sap that welled beneath the bark. Wasps were collecting ants which came to feed on the sap, and carrying them away as paralysed food for their storehouses. Bees hummed and frogs croaked, and in the trees the tiny tree spirits flitted about brighter than fireflies, brighter and livelier than Dreenee had ever seen them, and he wondered if they too were getting ready for the great Festival.

As Sun sat on the hilltops the women were busy around the campfires preparing for the feast. Dreenee wandered among the silver tussocks enjoying the glow of anticipation. Then to his amazement he heard his magpies calling him.

"Look and listen this way, Dreenee, look and listen this way!"

Quickly he scrambled down from the tree and hurried over to the place where the magpies had landed. He sat down quietly even though his legs were trembling, and they made a black and white circle around him, their intense eyes never leaving his face. A big old bird who was the leader stepped forward and spoke.

"Listen, Dreenee. Listen carefully. New Knowledge is coming into the camp tonight and you must hide and listen to every word and hold the words in your head, for they are very important. Sun has given to you the understanding of magpie-talk and made us your teachers. One day when you are bigger you will understand it all, but in the meantime you must follow where we lead you."

The small boy sat in a daze after the magpies had flown away. He did not want to return to the noisy camp for a little while so he wandered along the river, hoping to find some bright feathers or flowers to decorate his hair. Suddenly a bright parrot's feather floated down at his feet. Looking up he saw his magpies circling overhead, and each one was carrying a brightly coloured feather! As he watched, the feathers floated down at his feet and the magpies wheeled away down the river, warbling until they were out of sight. Gleefully Dreenee answered them with three beautiful peals of magpie-song. With wide unbelieving eyes he gathered up the feathers and arranging them in his hair, hurried down to the river to study his own reflection. In the fading light his shadow was long and the last rays of golden light shone on his feathers. They were all colours: red like fire, blue like the sky, and a beautiful green like the cherry tree!

Returning to camp, Dreenee was the centre of attention with so many bright feathers in his hair. Everyone wanted to know where he had found them. Then suddenly, three strange men walked into the camp. They asked for the Chief, and said they had come from the great Wide River in the south with news of two new ships which had arrived and did not go away.

Mannerganner called his men together and they moved away to receive the news. All eyes followed them as they squatted down. The women stopped laughing and talking, and even the little children seemed to sense that something was wrong.

Sun slipped quietly away and twilight walked softly in the Land. Birds settled for the night and around the campfire the women and children waited while the men talked together. All except Dreenee: he had made another magic circle around himself so that he could not be seen or heard and glided behind a big black log, close to the men.

Motionless he hid listening to every word the three men had to say about the two sailing ships which had not gone away and about the many pale-faced people who had come ashore and started cutting down trees and building large huts in the hunting grounds of Timtumele the wide river as it flows towards the sea. They had strange new animals with them and a new language, and they had terrible magic sticks which could kill from many many stones' throw away. Already they were killing *larner* with their magic sticks. Sometimes they even left the meat to rot, taking only the skins away. This had made the People of the Wide River very angry for no-one ever wasted good meat.

Dreenee saw fear and anger on every man's face as the New Knowledge was given. Mannerganner looked very troubled as he listened.

"Who is the Chief of these newcomers, that he could allow such a dreadful thing to happen?" he asked, and one of the men replied:

"His name is Bowen, and he calls our Land Van Diemen's Land." Everyone was astounded. There was no record of Van Diemen in the old legends which had been passed down. There must be some terrible mistake! This was Droemerdeene's Land, and it had been given to the People in the great Dreaming.

Mannerganner asked about the new animals, and the men told him that three creatures called 'cows' were brought ashore, and one creature called 'horse'. Also there were new birds called 'ducks' and 'hens' and there were were smaller animals called 'pigs' and 'sheep'. The strange men placed spears on the ground to explain how these new animals were held within 'fences'.

Dreenee listened and although he was so small he understood and remembered every word. He felt the fear and knew the danger which threatened his People.

Mannerganner then asked about the new people, and the three men said there seemed to be three types of pale-faced people. The ones wearing skins the colour of the mountain berry were called 'soldiers', who were in charge of other men called 'convicts', who wore skins the colour of storm-cloud. These men often had hard, heavy rope called 'chains' on their legs, which made it difficult for them to take big steps. The soldiers were very cruel to them, and beat them with 'whips' which looked like climbing ropes. Then there were several families who were called 'settlers'. They had new seeds and new food and new animals. Already they had started building huts and 'fences' to hold their new animals, and the convicts were made to work very hard making wide tracks and building 'bridges' over the rivers. Sometimes the soldiers drank brown water out of 'barrels' — round things like short tree trunks — and this seemed to make them even louder and very cruel. There was much fighting among the soldiers and they seemed to enjoy killing animals with their magic sticks and whipping the poor convicts. One of the convicts had already escaped into the bush and was living with the People of the Wide River. He was afraid of being caught again by the soldiers and he was afraid of starving in the bush, so he had made friends with the People. Already he had taught the People a lot about the habits and the language of the pale-faced newcomers, and they had taught him where to hide and where to find food.

The men talked for a long time as the twilight deepened. Then as *Wetar* began to climb over the hills, Mannerganner stood up and walked over to join the women and children and the young men around the huge campfire. Behind him came the three visitors from the Wide River and the council of wise men and last of all Dreenee slid silently from his hiding place and sat down beside his mother.

All eyes turned to *Wetar* as she climbed serene and radiant in a starlit sky, for she was ready to hear the songs of her People. Mannerganner gave the song of Droemerdeene to *Wetar*. Slowly the People took the rhythm of the song from Mannerganner as he stamped his feet and thumped his thighs. The tempo increased and the voices blended together, louder and louder; faster and faster; until the perspiration glowed on every face and dust rose from the ground. As Wetar climbed high the songs echoed in the hills and the smoke of the campfire cast long flickering shadows. Souls reached out in praise of Droemerdeene the great one, who had made the first black man and given him food; and Droemerdeene from his high place heard the song and came hopping through the golden blooms of draydee. He had the body of *larner* the kangaroo and the head of an Aborigine. For a moment he showed himself to the People and then softly he faded away.

The People sat quietly after Droemerdeene had faded. Fire crackled, crowding out the darkness, and they could feel the Old Ones very close. All eyes turned to the River of

Stars; each tiny star was the campfire of a loved one who had gone away. Slowly songs were sung for the Old Ones, and then songs for the little children. Afterwards there was much feasting and the three men who had come from the Wide River gave to the People of the Big River tribe a new dance. It was called the 'Horse Dance'. One man got down on his hands and knees and another man rode on his back. It told the story of the new animal called horse, which belonged to the chief named Bowen. It was a very popular dance and from that day became part of Common Knowledge. Many questions were asked about the new animals, especially horse. It was hard to imagine anyone sitting on the back of an animal and travelling without walking. Curiosity and fear mingled in the minds of the People as the three men gave the New Knowledge to the Big River tribe. The news filled them with foreboding for it brought the story of strange people who did not live according to the Law of the Land.

7. The Lawless Ones

News of the lawless Intruders spread fast through the Land and the People were confronted with Change.

Scouts were sent to the Wide River to look and listen, and returned to Mannerganner with incredible tales. The beautiful trees were being cut down and huts and fences built. It was not easy for them to explain these things to the councillors for they did not know about axes with handles, or saws or metal chains. Quite often the scouts used their hands and their voices to imitate the shape and the sound of these new things which were used for cutting down their living trees, and soon the people understood and became angry. Surely there was enough thick bark for building shelters?

In every camp the older men talked earnestly around their council fires, trying to find a reason for such strange behaviour, and finding none, their anger grew. Each day it became more obvious that they did not plan to go away again, like the other small parties who had come before them. The white men were killing more animals with their magic firesticks and their traps and snares, often only taking the skins. They were even digging up the soil and planting new seeds which they had brought with them, when everyone knew that Mother Earth supplied her own seeds. She also supplied the animals, yet they had brought new animals with them, and they were eating the grasses which belonged to *larner* the kangaroo and *gonnanner* the emu and *drogermutter* the wombat! Sheep and cows and horses did not belong to the Land.

Even in the special hunting grounds the wattles were being cut down to make walls for their homes and sheds for their animals, and beautiful peppermints were split into many pieces to make roofs and fences and bridges. There was even the story of the hut which was built from blocks of stone, yet close by there were caves which were much warmer. And what was more, they had named the place 'Risdon Cove'! Risdon Cove, when everyone knew it was Timtumele and it belonged to the Oyster Bay tribe!

The days grew longer as the older men collected and exchanged New Knowledge and made plans; and the younger hunters and warriors travelled backwards and forwards to the Wide River. With scouts from other bands they watched every move of the Intruders from the look-about hills which towered over the hunting grounds. Like bees they worked, collecting New Knowledge, and like bees they tirelessly returned to their camps and shared all they had collected with the leaders of their tribes, according to the Law.

The daily pattern changed also for the women and the children. They spent more time food-gathering alone, and less time lazing about under the trees and playing with their children. Even at night many of the men were often away. A new restlessness made them laugh too loudly and some-times fight among themselves. The little children could also feel the tension, brittle as dry bark beneath their feet as they travelled with their families as the ancient food-gathering cycle called them up over the great proud boulders to the Land of Many Lakes for the Egg Food Season. Twice *Wetar* the moon had grown thin as a peppermint leaf and then round and fat as the golden blossom of the wattle since the Festival of Droemerdeene, and in all that time the Intruders had not gone away. Nearly every day more news came into the camp and Dreenee would quickly make his magic hiding spell around himself and move close to Mannerganner. Sometimes he shivered with excitement when he heard the news from the scouts, and sometimes his big black eyes rolled about in their sockets as fear gripped him, but never did he make one sound; and never did the men know that he was listening to every word and understanding things which belonged only to the councillors.

It was full summer and sun shone warm in the Land of Many Lakes as the women and the children waded about in the shallow waters of the Lagoon of Islands, searching for eggs of *warrah* the duck and *kallerhoneyer* the swan. Dreenee frolicked about with his little friends, sometimes throwing stones and sometimes playing hiding and stalking games, as the women pushed their way through the reeds. Now and then a startled bird whirred into the sunlight and there would be a laughing noisy race through the silver-soft waters to the place where she had been sitting on her eggs.

Ningermaner sat in the shade of a cherry tree, contentedly watching her People as her nimble fingers twisted a bundle of wet reeds into another new basket. Beside her, Longameena's new girl-child sucked noisily on a tiny plumbrown fist, and nearby two old men dozed in the warmth of the sun. Softly she crooned the Song of the Family as she watched the children and worked on her basket. It was good to see the children playing so well together. The lagoon made a wonderful playground and school. There were so many places for hiding and stalking games among the reeds, and there were sitting-still places where they could listen to the music of the water spirits, or the message of Wind as it sighed softly in the sunlight. Fondly the old woman smiled to herself as she watched Dreenee giving the orders. Already children older than himself were playing the game the way he planned it.

Suddenly a colony of magpies flew low over the reeds where the children played and Ningermaner followed them with her eyes as they circled. When next she looked to the place where Dreenee had been playing, he had completely vanished. The older children were at first bewildered and then laughingly they began to search for Dreenee the clever one, who surely must be hiding. But Ningermaner knew better. Already her shoulder was twitching. As she listened to her help-spirits with her inside ear, the warmth went out of the day. More news had come into the camp, and it was not good news.

8. The White Sticks

Dreenee sat close to the councillors, completely hidden in his magic circle, as Mannerganner received the news from his scouts. More ships had sailed up the Wide River and more Intruders had come ashore. The hunting grounds, on both sides of the rivers, were now crawling with long lines of men and a few women and children. Like ants, they flowed out of the ships with their endless supply of possessions. From the lookabout hills the scouts had watched as soldiers herded more convicts ashore. They heard the rattle of the chains on their legs and the angry new language of the soldiers. Magic firesticks glinted from their shoulders, and whips as long as climbing ropes flicked and cracked fiercely at the struggling line of convicts. Sometimes the man named Bowen rode about on his horse, giving orders, and sometimes they saw him taking orders from a much older new man, dressed in very bright clothes. He seemed to be their new Chief. Like mushrooms, more white tents sprang up; the features of the hunting grounds were completely changing. Where only five moons ago the slopes had been covered with soft green bushes and towering trees, now there were huts and tents, fences and new animals and new people.

Dreenee listened to every word, understanding all that was said and storing it in his mind as Mannerganner and his councillors asked many questions. Soon with his inside eye he could see beyond the ranges and into the faraway hunting ground of the Wide River People, where the lawless ones swarmed like bees. It was a new and frightening time for the little boy, and he was glad when the vision had faded away and he looked up into the tree where his magpies sat. His eyes met the bright red eyes of the leader and presently the old bird spoke: "Listen and remember, Dreenee. Listen and remember. One day you will be Man, but now you must remember all you have heard and seen, but speak not of it. Go now and become a leader among the children. Teach them cunning ways. Teach them to run swiftly and hide well. Practise with them stone-throwing so your arms will be strong and your aim straight to throw the spear of a warrior, for one day many of your People will depend on you."

Dreenee waded out from behind a log and the children yelled and squealed with delight. Soon they were racing around the shore, following him to the place where the stones were smooth and round. Here they played his stone-throwing game until Sun began to wink and slide away, and hunger drew them towards the sharp smell of meat roasting on the glowing fires, back along the lake shore.

As summer grew stronger the scouts returned again and again to the Wide River. The new Leader whose name was 'Collins' called the place 'Hobart Town'; and the newcomers were spreading out along the riverbanks. They had a strange habit of driving white sticks of wood into the ground and, wherever the white sticks stood, very soon soldiers arrived with gangs of convicts and began cutting down the trees and building huts and fences. The white sticks, they began to realise, were something to do with white man's tribal boundaries, and so plans were made to pull them out.

One afternoon two warriors had just snatched away a white stick to take home to their councillors when a dreadful booming noise, louder than thunder, whistled past them. The other warriors who were keeping watch sprang into action and raced down towards the soldiers with their spears. Again the noise like thunder boomed, so the warriors retreated to a high place where they hurled rocks and stones at the white men until night closed in. When the first light of dawn crept into their camp, scouts left to carry the news back to their various bands. Even though no-one was hurt, it was a bad sign. No longer could the newcomers be trusted. In the beginning the looking and listening had been mostly out of curiosity. Then fear had grown. Now there was deep anger.

Twice *Wetar* waxed and waned as more New Knowledge was added, but it was not until Autumn began to fade into Winter that the most alarming news of all was brought before the councillors. People of the Oyster Bay tribe had been attacked at Timtumele! Men, women and children had been killed with the terrible magic firesticks when they had been hunting *larner*, their own food in their own hunting ground!

Scouts and warriors were ordered to continue collecting New Knowledge, but they were warned about the lawbreakers. No longer could the newcomers be trusted, or allowed to share the food and shelter which Mother Earth provided. The people began spearing the sheep which were eating the grasses belonging to their own animals and they burnt down huts and bridges. There was no other way, for the councillors could see that soon whole tribes would be driven out of their own hunting grounds and would themselves become law-breakers among their own People, and then they could expect to be punished according to the Law.

Every time Mannerganner called his councillors together, Dreenee, his magic hiding circle around him, learnt about the ways of the trappers and the shooters and the timber cutters and about bushrangers. Soon there was news of stockkeepers who followed small herds of cattle from place to place. They were considered very dangerous and often attacked People for no reason at all. Settlers were spreading out and building more huts and fences. They had bullocks to pull their waggons, and later they had sheep and cattle. They even had things called 'ploughs' which the bullocks pulled, cutting deep into Mother Earth and where they were dragged, strange new plants soon grew. The small boy's head was full of New Knowledge, yet he could not share it with the women and children. He could not talk about it to anyone except his magpies, so when he was not romping about with the other children, or teaching them stone-throwing and cunning ways, he would sit alone by some little creek and talk to the tiny waterspirits who danced there, or simply climb into a tree where the tree-spirits lived; and usually his magpies would arrive and settle down to talk with him.

9. The Beginning of Change

Every season brought more news and much of it was later given to the women and children and younger men by one of the wise Songmen. Nearly every night around the fire Dreenee would hear again some of the inside news he had collected from his magpies or from the councillors.

Some of the news made most amusing songs and dances and soon became favourites of the women and children, especially the one about the newcomer who got lost in the bush and couldn't even retrace his own lugga back to his camp. And the family who built their hut too close to the river and were washed away when the river swelled with rain in the middle of the night! How the women had laughed! Even the little children had rolled over, laughing, as the story was told in song and dance. But there were other customs which were too incredible to talk about even in a whisper.

One story seemed to make no sense at all. Some days seemed different. A bell rang and the white people at Hobart Town went inside a building. They stood in straight rows, singing songs, and then they sat very quietly and stared up at the leader, whose name was 'Knopwood'; and listened very seriously while he talked about this God. The wisest of the councillors said that 'God' must be an Ancestral Being and the People accepted this New Knowledge; yet they could not understand the strange custom of worshipping inside a building with a roof on top which must surely block out the sun, the moon and the stars. And they could not understand why the pale-faced ones only went into the building when the bell rang. Perhaps their God only visited them on certain days? They felt sorry for the newcomers who were not surrounded all the time by their Ancestral Beings. This was probably the reason why they fought so much and betrayed one another and drank the evil stuff called rum from wooden barrels. The soldiers seemed to enjoy whipping convicts and often women and children crowded round to watch one of their own countrymen whipped, or even hung by the neck until he was dead.

In the winter while the People were in the Seafood Land, several more ships arrived at Hobart Town and then one day news came of two ships which had arrived in another river at the top of the island. Another settlement sprang up almost overnight, and was named 'Port Dalrymple' when all the People knew its proper name was Panatana.

Dreenee shivered when he heard the news. Although he had never been to Panatana he could see (very faintly with his inside eye) the lovely estuary being invaded and the Intruders slowly spreading out along its banks. It was a lot of bad news for one young boy to hold in his head, so he was glad when the councillors stood up and walked away to their sleeping places and he could go to Ningermaner.

Every night Dreenee loved to sleep close to his grandmother, because he knew she could think his thoughts, and when he had almost too much unhappy news to handle alone, it was nice to feel her close to him. Sometimes he had a little gift for her tucked in his tight woolly curls and sometimes she had something for him in the small pouch she wore suspended around her neck, but they never talked about inside news. There was no need. He could feel it flowing into Ningermaner's mind, by simply being close to her. He could almost open his inside ear and hear what she was thinking — but not quite. His magic powers were growing stronger every day and he knew that it wouldn't be long before he could listen to her thoughts. Already they were a soft muffled whisper. Perhaps one day his magic would be stronger than his grandmother's and he could keep her out of his head; but just for now it was a nice warm feeling to share his thoughts with her. There was news of burning down of huts and shooting of warriors and spearing of white people. There was even the dreadful story of the tiny baby who had been thrown on the camp fire and burnt alive because its father had speared a sheep. Dreenee had shivered and shuddered so badly when the news was given that he could not hold his magic circle together any longer. He simply had to get close to Ningermaner before his whole body burst with such terrible news.

When he hurled himself down beside her he sobbed and sobbed, until gently she took away the pain and he slept, a deep dreamless sleep of exhaustion.

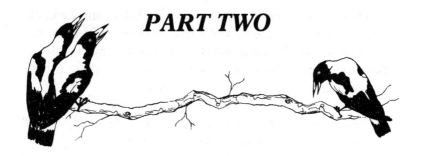

PART TWO

10. Following Horse

Dawn was casting a rosy hue over Droemerdeene's Land as Dreenee slipped away from camp.

He was eating the small red berries of the wild cherry tree when he heard the urgent Travel Song of his magpies.

Forgetting about food, Dreenee hurtled down the gully until he came to a creek. Here on the banks his magpies waited for him. They were very excited, so Dreenee looked at the trees and looked at Sky, but could see nothing, so he studied the ground and noticed tracks in the mud. Kangaroo and wombat had been here earlier, but there was also a new track very large and deep. It was made before last night's frost, and was almost a circle!

Circles were very important to the People. They belonged to Sacred Knowledge. Perhaps this new animal was sacred!

Over the next hill and into the next gully, Dreenee followed the new tracks and overhead the magpies flew warbling excitedly. Soon they came to a place where the little creek fed the Fat Doe River, and here the birds perched high in a yellow gumtree.

Dreenee clambered up a tree and there ahead he could see a strange new animal. It was the largest he had ever seen — the colour of the big kangaroo. It had a short hairy coat and it stood on its four legs. Its tail was of long black hair which hung down nearly to the ground and there was more long black hair along its neck. As the young boy watched, the animal quietly cropped the grasses.

Sometimes its tail swished across its back, and he could tell that it was female — yet it had no pouch. Dreenee was fascinated! He slithered down the tree and moved closer to the new animal. Most of the animals he knew carried their young in pouches.

A breeze carried the first scent of the new animal to him. "Wah! Wah!" he called out excitedly to the magpies and the creature, hearing him, snorted and moved away. As it did so, he heard a clanging noise like chipping of flints and he realised that the two front legs had a short rope-thing between them.

Many small birds came to drink at the creek but Dreenee did not notice them. Fascinated, he kept his eyes fixed on the beautiful new animal. Soon she stopped walking and started to eat again.

Suddenly she raised her head and her ears pricked forward. Looking in the same direction, Dreenee saw a white man approaching. He walked towards the animal carrying something like a climbing rope.

The animal waited and the man came up to her and put part of the rope around her head. Then the animal made a new noise, a soft drawn-out sound not at all like the snort of fear. The man patted the animal and then removed the ropes from her front legs and sprang on to the middle of her back! Dreenee could not believe his eyes as the man and animal moved away. They seemed to be moving together like friends! They moved away slowly. Then the animal changed her foot pattern and they disappeared around the next bend of the river.

Dreenee wanted to race after the new animal, but the magpies fluttered down around him. Their eyes looked very stern as they stared at him and they moved even closer. He knew he must remain, for he could feel they were trying to give him a new word.

He closed his eyes and ears. To his mind came the memory of the Horse Dance which had been added to Common Knowledge when the first horse arrived in Droemerdeene's Land.

44

"Horse?" he laughed aloud. Away flew the magpies in the direction of camp.

"Thank you, maggy magpies", he called.

"Horse", he said. Dreenee traced the shape of the footprints in the mud and stored them in his mind. They were hard, bony ones — quite different from the soft padded feet of the only other animals he knew. He found the place where Horse had stood earlier in the day and the place where Horse had slept. Here Dreenee also lay down, filling his nostrils with the sweet new smell which hung on the long flattened grasses. Somehow, one day, he must find Horse again and make friends. It would be wonderful to ride on her back and travel faster than the kangaroo! There would be so many new places that he could show Horse!

Back in camp Dreenee told the women what he had seen. As usual he was scolded for going off alone. The men heard every word and although they said nothing, the young boy noticed two men leave the camp and he knew instinctively that Mannerganner had sent them to look and listen.

Next night around the campfire Mannerganner had something new to add to Common Knowledge. The men had returned after a long day of looking and listening to tell him about a settlement of the white people on the morning side of the Wide River, half a day's walk away. Trees had been cut down and several huts built. Some were made of wood and there was one long low hut made of rough stones. There was also a fence made out of peppermint gums and inside the fence were some of the white man's new animals. A man and a woman and two children lived there.

Dreenee listened quietly, for he was thinking and planning. Moonah, seeing his eyes, knew that she would need to keep a very close watch over her son. He was growing far too curious about things which did not concern him.

11. Dreenee is Captured

All night Dreenee had tossed restlessly. When he did sleep, his dreams were full of beautiful Horse. At first light he moved stealthily from his sleeping place.

Following Horse's tracks he arrived on the brow of a hill and looking down saw the white man's house. Horse was not in the yard but a woman was bending over a bush of bright flowers while two children frolicked nearby.

Dreenee stood watching, and his curiosity overpowered his caution. He did not take care. He had forgotten the important rule of listening and looking behind him.

Suddenly a man appeared. He was being carried on Horse's back.

Dreenee started to run, but it was hopeless. The man and Horse were coming closer. He could now hear the heavy breathing of Horse. Thinking he was about to be killed, he grabbed a few stones to throw at the man; but it was too late. They were now too close.

Dreenee tried dodging, but it was no good. Quickly the man bent down from Horse and pulled Dreenee up in front of him. The young boy had never been so close to a pale-skinned man and he thrashed about with his arms and legs, terrified. Horse lunged and reared, but still the man held him. He even laughed as he urged horse forward down the hill and into the yard.

Here the man called to his family in their strange new language and the woman appeared with the two children beside her. The boy was Dreenee's size and the girl was smaller. She had big blue eyes and most beautiful hair, the colour of setting Sun and *ballawinne* the red ochre.

Everyone stared at Dreenee.

Inside the house Dreenee was tied to a chair. He was given some food by the woman, but for once in his life he wasn't hungry. The pale-skinned boy laughed as Dreenee screwed up his face at the food and wouldn't eat. The girl simply stared at him with big blue eyes.

Soon the man came into the room again with a tub of hot, steaming water. The only hot water Dreenee had seen was used by the sealers for cooking crayfish. Surely they were not going to cook him! Dreenee's heart pounded. Somehow he must not let his fear show. He must use all his cunning, he thought. So he smiled as though he were enjoying himself. If he could trick them into thinking he liked being here perhaps they wouldn't tie him to the chair again. It was the most hateful thing that had ever happened to him; much worse than being put in a tree and jeered at.

The children put their hands in the water, smiling at him, and the boy said 'Bath'. The man untied Dreenee and gently helped him up.

Smiling through his fear, Dreenee put his hand and then one foot in the water and much to his surprise found that it was really no hotter than a rock pool in summer. Then he put the other foot in and, sitting down, smiled at everyone.

The man handed him some soap. He smelt it and liked the smell. So he tasted it and that made everyone laugh. It was not nice being laughed at but he continued to look pleased, even though the soap tasted awful. The man showed him how to use soap and soon his skin felt quite different. Even the water looked different; it was now brown and greasy.

In a daze he felt his body being dried. Then someone put a bright shirt over his head. Next his legs were pushed into trousers. He didn't like the scratchy feel of trousers but he still managed to smile. However, it was simply too much when his feet were put into boots. How could he ever run away with these terrible, stiff things on his feet? He had had more than enough. He yelled loudly and tried to kick the boy, so the boots were quickly put aside and once again the woman offered him food.

He had heard through Common Knowledge about poisons which the Intruders put in flour and sugar and so he knew that it could be dangerous to eat the food, but then he had also heard of Intruders who stole children to work for them. If these people had stolen him for this work, he was almost sure they would not kill him.

Carefully he took the bread and passed it to the boy. The boy ate some, so Dreenee tasted it. He didn't like the butter on top of it, but the bread tasted quite nice so he scraped the butter off. It seemed natural to rub it into his hair but everyone laughed loudly when he did so and poor Dreenee felt utterly confused and close to tears. He hung his head. "Moonah, Moonah, Ningermaner", he sobbed.

The boy sensed Dreenee's unhappiness so he pointed to himself and said "Thomas". Then he pointed to the little girl and said "Alice", so Dreenee pointed to himself and said "Dreenee". He felt better. Names were very important.

For the rest of the day Dreenee stayed in the room with some of the family. Sometimes one or two of them would go out through the door but he was never left alone. He smiled nearly all the time and soon his face was tired with smiling, but it was better than being tied in a chair.

He could see many things. On the mantelpiece over the fireplace something went 'tick-tock' but it was not a beetle. The noise came from a shiny thing. Thomas, seeing his curiosity, showed him the hands slowly moving and gave him the word 'Time'. The long finger went quite fast and the short finger very slowly. Time really was interesting but what use did it have?

On a table there were books and they fascinated Dreenee. Seeing his interest, the children showed him one. In no time he had learnt to turn the pages and look at the pictures. Most of them showed animals, some of which he knew, and soon he was saying his names for them and Thomas was saying his names, though they both found the other's words very difficult to pronounce.

Soon they were all laughing together. Thomas and Alice, Dreenee thought, really were fun to be with even though their skins were pale and their smell most unusual. And Alice's hair was beautiful!

Dreenee walked around the room studying the furniture and the things hanging on the walls and over the fireplace.

He smelt and touched things as he moved about and the children and their father watched him. Quite often they talked together in their own strange language. There was wood in the fireplace but it wasn't alight. Seeing Dreenee's interest, the man came over and, taking a stone thing from his pocket, rubbed the two rough edges together. Suddenly there was fire! Dreenee's eyes were almost popping out of his head as he watched the wood crackle and spark! The man had made Fire! It was something to do with the metal things. Somehow he must find out more about the metal things. How excited the men would be if he could teach them how to make Fire! There would be no need to carry firesticks on their journeys!

Dreenee walked over to the window again. He could think better if he were looking at his hills. He needed time to think about this New Knowledge. When he looked out of the window he could not believe his eyes. A woman was bringing in clothes from the line but she was not a pale-skinned one. She was dark! She belonged to his People!

There she was, all dressed up in the white people's clothes. Even her hair was long like a man's hair and not shaved off as was the custom among the women; and she had those dreadful things on her feet! He had forgotten all about Time and Fire because he was so amazed.

"Wah! Wah!" he yelled, pointing to the woman, and Thomas came over to stand beside him.

"That is Maria", he said.

"Maria?" Dreenee replied, thinking to himself that 'Maria' did not sound at all like a tribal name. "Maria?" he said again, finding it a difficult word to remember, yet trying to store it in his mind.

Suddenly Thomas' father took his arm and led him outside along the path to another room where there was already a fire burning.

"Time for bed", he said. He patted Dreenee kindly and went outside.

Dreenee could hear the door click shut and the sound of the man's footsteps moving away. He did not like being left alone. In all his life he had never been alone at night.

The windows had bars across them and the roof was too high for him to reach. He tried to open the door but it was tightly shut. It would not budge even though he pulled and pushed with all his might. Dreenee felt trapped.

He could already see that Sun was walking away behind the hills and soon the only light would come from Fire. He huddled down beside it feeling utterly miserable. He wondered if he should set fire to the room but soon realised that this would be dangerous. He might get burnt himself. Instead he studied all the strange new things.

A table stood in the corner and on it was a pannikin of water and some bread, which he recognised, and carrots and apples, which he did not. He smelt them and looked at them, but didn't eat any. It seemed to Dreenee that for the first time in his life he was not hungry.

There were many curious things in the room, but Dreenee couldn't understand what use they had.

A large bag stood in the corner, and inside it were some strange seeds. They were larger than sag corn seed that the People ground on their flat stones but tasted much the same. He crunched a few grains in his strong white teeth and felt better. It was easier to think when he was chewing something, so he took a handful of seeds and sat on the floor close to the fire. Nearby a sheepskin mat caught his attention, so he picked it up and turned it over. It was an animal skin, he realised, but one he hadn't seen before. It was about the same size as a kangaroo skin but so much thicker and warmer. Dreenee even liked the smell of it so he curled himself up on the soft sheepskin and tried to plan his escape; but he felt very lonely and closed in, with four walls round him and a roof overhead. He couldn't see the stars or the shadows of the trees and most of all he couldn't hear the laughter of his People.

Tired and confused, Dreenee drifted off into sleep. It had been a long and terrifying day.

12. New Ways

Dreenee woke next morning to the call of the magpies. He sprang to his feet, wondering where he was. He rushed to the window and peered out, looking for his magpies.

In the early half-light he could just see them. They were perched in a nearby tree, looking intently at the window. It was not a normal, happy sunrise song that they were singing; it was an urgent call and Dreenee knew they were trying to tell him something. It was something to do with escaping — but what? He was desperate. They were too far away for their plan to flow into his head.

"Come closer", he pleaded, and very soon the leader fluttered down from the tree and settled just outside the window. He scratched about in the grass, warbling softly. His eyes were very bright. Now and then he paused and looked through the window.

"The smoke hole!" the magpie seemed to say. "Climb up the smoke hole."

"Wah! Wah! Thank you, maggy magpie! Wait for me — I'm coming now!"

He rushed over to the fireplace and looked up. Yes! He could just see daylight. The fire had gone out but the stones were still rather hot. Not too hot, he decided. And the size was just right and there were lots of rough edges to grip.

"Wait for me, maggy magpie", he called softly, with a broad grin on his face. Then suddenly the smile faded. He could hear the sound of footsteps coming closer; a heavy one and two light skipping ones and then the noise of the opening of the door.

"Oh, no! It's too late. I can't come now", he almost whimpered.

Dreenee put on his best smile, knowing that he would have a lot of acting to do today, even though he was still afraid. He even offered his half-eaten carrot to Alice and everyone went happily out of the hut and along the flagstone path to the big kitchen.

51

He thought of making a dash for the hills, for no-one was holding on to him, but then he remembered the awful trousers. They would make running difficult. He decided to wait. Another day would give him the chance to learn more about the ways of the strangers, especially Time and Fire and Maria.

For Dreenee the kitchen was a fascinating place. There were new things everywhere. Over the fire hung pots on hooks and nice smells were coming from them.

He was busy peering into pots when he heard footsteps coming along the flagstones. He turned round to find two big brown eyes staring at him. It was Maria!

"Wah! Wah!", he said in greeting to her.

A bewildered smile swept across her face and he could tell she was pleased to see him; and very surprised.

When she spoke Dreenee knew that she belonged to another tribe because he could barely understand her, but she was so beautiful that it didn't really matter. In spite of the peculiar clothes she wore, and her strange long hair, she was simply lovely. He wondered which tribe she belonged to. Ningermaner and Mannerganner would know, of course, but Dreenee was too young. So far he only knew the speech of the Oyster Bay tribe and his own Big River tribe.

Dreenee was still gazing at Maria when Thomas came over and led him to the table. Bowls of hot porridge were put in front of each of them by Maria, who then sat down opposite Dreenee. He copied her as she picked up the spoon and ate her porridge. All eyes were on him as he held the spoon and tasted the new food.

It was good. He was very hungry, so when he had finished he started to eat the sugar out of the sugar bowl! Nearly everyone laughed, which puzzled poor Dreenee. Slowly a tear rolled down his face. The man and the woman were laughing at him and Thomas was laughing too, but not Maria, nor little Alice. The little girl sat gazing at him with her big blue eyes. When she saw his tears, she passed him a piece of stuff with pretty flowers on it and showed him how to wipe away his tears. Then Alice helped him put the 'hanky' in his 'pocket'. At the fire, Maria was taking eggs out of a basket and dropping them carefully into a pot containing water which was bubbling and steaming. After a few minutes she took the eggs out of the pot and brought them to the table. They still had their shells on, but they were hot — really hot.

Dreenee was fascinated. He watched the family put them in little cups and begin to eat the solid yellow and white food. It did not look slippery like the raw eggs of duck and native hen. Dreenee ate his first egg, copying Alice. It was delicious! He went over to where Maria was cooking more eggs and she allowed him to choose one from the basket and put it in the water.

Five times Dreenee ate an egg and went back for another. Everyone watched with amazement! He was the centre of attention and he rather enjoyed it. He could eat more eggs than anyone, even the big man! He beamed his biggest and best smile at everyone.

After breakfast the man took Dreenee outside with Thomas and Alice. Inside the gumtree fence were several little sheds and huts. Dreenee was shown inside each one.

In one hut some big black birds were given seeds that looked rather like sag corn.

"Hens", Thomas said, as he showed Dreenee their nests full of straw and handed him a warm egg to feel.

Dreenee didn't want to give the egg back and tried to put it in his pocket, but Thomas shook his head, saying "No". Confused, Dreenee handed back the egg, thinking how strange it was to shut birds away in a hut.

The next shed was even more exciting and, at first, frightening. There stood Horse, watching them with big brown eyes! It was the one which had carried him away yesterday!

The three children stood together as the man took some stuff out of a wooden bin and put it in a box in the corner. It looked like chopped up summer grass and smelt like it, too. Horse was soon munching away at the food. The children patted Horse and Dreenee copied them. He loved the warm soft feel and the smell of Horse.

Further down the yard were two big animals, nearly as big as Horse, and several much smaller ones. They were all quietly eating grass, and Dreenee soon learnt they were called 'Cow' and 'Sheep'. Both cows had bony things between their ears which curled forward and were pointy. Dreenee had never seen an animal with bone outside its skin, so he pointed and Thomas gave him the word 'horn' and, putting his head down playfully, showed Dreenee how horns were used. It became quite a joke as they pretended to be cows horning each other and Dreenee realised that horns could be useful — almost as useful as legs for kicking.

Dreenee was now very curious about Sheep. He wanted to touch one but they stopped eating grass and trotted away in a tight little mob, so Thomas and Alice pushed them into a corner and then Dreenee was able to feel one of them.

"Wah! Wah!", he said, as he felt again the same soft warm feeling and knew that it was a sheep's skin that he had slept on last night.

While everyone was laughing, the woman came over carrying a container. Her eyes were smiling as she put her hand on the sheep's back, and told Dreenee that sheep grew wool and people made wool into warm clothes and blankets. So many words didn't make much sense for Dreenee, but when Thomas touched his own woolly jumper and then the sheep, and said "Wool — Sheep's wool", Dreenee began to understand. He wondered how the wool got off the sheep and into a jumper, but it didn't really matter. The woman was already busy sitting down close to Cow, and he could hear a splashing noise.

Dreenee soon forgot about wool. His whole attention now became fixed on what the woman was doing. None of his People ever thought of carrying milk around in a bucket. The only milk he knew was for babies and young animals in pouches. Yet these people carried milk inside their houses and put it on their porridge! It was, he thought, a clever idea.

While Dreenee watched the woman milking Cow, the man came round the corner leading Horse. He went over to a small hut from inside which Dreenee could hear a yapping sound. The man opened the door and out bounded a little animal.

It was bigger than a devil-dog but much the same shape, and it ran to each of the children and licked their arms and legs, and even tried to lick Dreenee's face! Thomas and Alice were not afraid of the bounding whirling animal which never stopped wagging its tail and yapping. It was a happy creature and Thomas told Dreenee its name was 'Patches'. Dreenee had heard about Dog through Common Knowledge.

Suddenly the man whistled, and Dog stopped playing with the children and bounded away towards him. There the man sprang on to Horse and rode away down the gully, with Dog running along behind him.

As Dreenee watched Man and Horse and Dog disappear over the hill, the woman came over with the bucket of milk, and they all walked along the stone path towards the house.

Near the back door was a thing with wood burning under it. Dreenee had seen it before at the sealers' camp, but not so close and he felt he must look into it. Here clothes were bubbling in hot water! The whole idea was fascinating. What a lot of work clothes made, he wanted to say, but of course no-one would understand him, and Thomas was talking to him.

"Come on, Dreenee. Time for bread and jam and milk."

Dreenee already knew bread and milk, but he wondered what jam was. The very thought of more new food made him smile. He had forgotten all about clothes as he followed the people.

Not far away he could see Maria standing beside a round wooden thing. Water ran out of it into a bucket. Dreenee was very curious to see the thing which held the water. The only water he knew tumbled along in the rivers, or lay still in the lagoons, and of course there was Sea. Water was very important. Later he must find out more about the thing holding the water and he wanted to talk to Maria too. Again Thomas spoke:

"Time for bread and jam and milk."

So Dreenee followed them into the house, trying to remember all the new words, especially Time.

"Time, Time", thought Dreenee. "Whatever was Time?" He had already heard the word many times.

Looking out of the kitchen window, Dreenee could see Maria hanging clothes out to dry, and he wanted to know more about her. He wished she would come inside, for he had a wonderful idea. Perhaps he could get her up the smoke-hole and take her home to his people, but he was not sure if she would fit. And it would not be easy to explain his plan without the white ones finding out. Even now Thomas and Alice were staring at him. He hoped they could not hear his thoughts. He emptied his head of escape plans and concentrated on eating the lovely soft food.

Presently Maria came into the kitchen. Her face lit up when she saw Dreenee again, and she patted him on the head.

"Maria", he said with a broad grin, but much to his amazement the smile faded quickly on her face. She scowled, stamping her foot.

"No!" she said, "Pungertenner", pointing to herself.

Dreenee now had so much New Knowledge to hold in his head, that he knew he would have to use all his cunning to keep it there, so he pretended to be tired and curled up on the floor near the fire. No-one seemed to mind.

Keeping his eyelids mere slits, he watched everything, yet at the same time he went over the New Knowledge he had gained, trying to fix in his mind all the new sights and sounds and smells. And he thought too about Pungertenner. It was a beautiful name; and so much easier to remember than Maria!

He watched her peeling potatoes and carrots and putting them in pots of hot water. Several times he saw her look in his direction and instinctively he felt that she knew he was peeping through his long black eyelashes, for she had a faraway secret smile on her face, and sometimes she sang as she moved about the kitchen. He even wondered if she could open her inside ear and listen to his thinking, like Ningermaner and his magpies.

If only Ningermaner were here, he thought, she would probably know where Pungertenner came from, and how he could help her to escape. Already he had decided that she was too big to climb up the smoke-hole. There was only just enough room for someone his size.

The smell of dinner cooking mingled with all the other nice smells as Dreenee listened to the song and pretended to sleep. Three times he heard a booming noise. Now he heard it again, almost like thunder; yet outside it was a sunny day. Then he heard the drumming sound of Horse's feet and so he opened his eyes and stretched himself, pretending to wake.

Looking out of the window he saw the man tie Horse to the fence and then hang two dead swans upside down in the tree!

"*Kallerhoneyer*! *Kallerhoneyer*!" Dreenee said, looking straight at Pungertenner, but she did not know the Big River word for 'swan'. "*Ropettener*", she said thoughtfully, in her own dialect.

The man came inside carrying a bag and put it on the bench. Everyone clustered around him as he emptied the contents into two tin dishes and covered them with water. Three dead eels were coiled in the bottom of one dish and several mountain trout lay in the other dish.

Dreenee was horrifed to see the fish. Eel was nice to eat, but the fish! Surely these people were not going to eat fish with scales! It was the Law never to eat fish with scales.

Thomas turned a fish over in his hands and passed one to Dreenee, saying "Fish", but the Aboriginal boy scowled and moved away. He looked to Pungertenner wondering what she thought, but she had closed her mind. Her eyes were busy as she took hot potatoes and hot carrots out of pots and put them on plates with mutton. Dreenee really enjoyed the meal, especially the meat. It was the tastiest meat he had ever eaten and he wanted to know more about it, so he picked up a piece and, looking straight at Pungertenner, said, "New Meat?"

"Yes, Dreenee", she said, "Sheep."

After dinner everyone went outside and sat under a big white gumtree — all except Pungertenner. As Dreenee walked away he noticed Pungertenner pile up the empty plates and begin to wash them with hot water. What a lot of work pots and plates must make for these pale-faced people, he thought, as he sat down with Thomas and Alice under the tree.

The man, he noticed, was smoking a pipe and the woman was joining two pieces of cloth together with a bright red thread. This was something he had never seen before. His People had no reason to do it but it was a very interesting idea. He must learn more about this later, but first he must know how the man killed the swans.

He moved closer to study the swans. Blood had dropped from a hole in each head, so he knew they had not been pulled under the water and drowned. Stones could not make a small hole like that, and neither could a spear. It must be something to do with the booming noise and the strange stick the man had carried.

His head full of New Knowledge, and his stomach full of good food, Dreenee's thoughts slowly drifted. He could feel sleep washing over him and carrying him away. Sun was warm and he was no longer afraid of these people. Tonight, if he were lucky, he might get up the smoke-hole and then run home to his People. He closed his eyes and fell asleep almost at once.

13. Time on His Hands

Sun had travelled right across the top of Sky while Dreenee slept, and when he opened his eyes he was looking straight at Dog. Patches was licking his face!

Startled, he bounded to his feet, trying to remember where he was, and Dog nearly pushed him over as it frolicked about, wagging its tail, yapping at him. Dog was not shy like the tiger-wolf; or cringing and snarling like the devil-dog. Dog was fun!

Perhaps he could take Patches back to camp? It would be nice to have his own special friend. But even as the young boy thought over the idea he knew that the women would not allow him to keep Dog. A pot might please the women; and he knew Pungertenner would definitely please everyone. A sheepskin would please Ningermaner; it would be very light to carry.

In front of the house Dreenee could see the woman digging holes in the ground and putting small trees in the holes. Surely he must be dreaming? Why would anyone do this? He watched her until he heard a banging noise come from a hut, and he could now see the big man on the roof. Sometimes he took little things out of his pocket and held them in his lips while he banged on the roof.

Dreenee walked over to the hut and stood watching. The man threw one of the strange things down to him.

"Nail", he said, and smiled as he watched Dreenee look intently at it, saying "Nail, Nail" and put it in his pocket with Hanky.

Dreenee's head was almost bursting with so much New Knowledge. His People did not plant trees and they did not use nails to keep their bark huts from falling down.

Thoughtfully he looked about and couldn't see Thomas or Alice, so he wandered over to watch the woman. She had a digging-stick, but it was different from the People's simple digging-sticks. It had a place for the foot to push it

59

down. The woman smiled as he studied the digging-stick, and she showed him how to use it.

"Dreenee is digging", she said very slowly. He beamed back at her, repeating the word "digging, digging", pleased with himself as he pushed the digging-stick into the ground and turned the soil over.

In doing so the spade split open a rotten root and several large yellow grubs wriggled out. Eagerly Dreenee gathered them up. First he ate one to show the woman it was good and then he handed one to her; but much to his surprise she shook her head.

"No, thank you", she said.

'No' he understood, but whatever could 'thank you' mean?

"Thank you, thank you", he said, enjoying the new word. Perhaps it was their word for this sort of grub!

Dreenee soon forgot about digging when Horse appeared with Thomas and Alice on its back. Two children on Horse! He wondered if there would be room for three.

"Dreenee Horse", he said, beaming all over his face and jumping for joy. Everyone laughed, and soon the woman was helping Alice down. Then she lifted him up in front of Thomas.

Dreenee was beside himself with joy! It was such a warm soft place on Horse, and he was so high up. He could even see over the fence and down to the river!

Round and round the yard the two boys rode, past the two cows, in and out among the gumtrees and huts and all the time Dreenee smiled and soaked up the feel and smell and movement and sound of Horse.

Under a tree he could see Pungertenner with a container of hot water. Every time they rode past her she smiled at him. She was pulling the feathers from the two dead swans.

Why, he wondered, would anyone want to pull out the feathers? His People put birds straight on the fire, feathers and all.

It seemed to Dreenee that Pungertenner was always working, when she should be laughing. The sooner he got her back with her own People the better. Too many women had already been stolen.

Presently the man came over to put Horse away. He lifted Dreenee down and allowed him to lead her into the hut.

"Time for the Horse to eat", said Thomas.

There was that word 'Time' again, and another new word! He did not know what 'Eat' meant.

"Eat?" he said, and Alice opened her mouth and pretended to eat while Thomas filled Horse's box with chaff and said "Horse is eating".

'Eat' he now knew, but 'Time' he still could not understand. Maybe Pungertenner could explain.

He slipped away while the others were busy with Horse. He wanted to be alone while he talked to Pungertenner. He wanted so badly to tell her of his wonderful escape plan and find out more about Time.

"Wah! Wah! Pungertenner", he said. Before he could say more, Thomas and Alice appeared.

"Time to eat, Dreenee", Alice said, leading him away.

"Time?" he asked, looking into her pale blue eyes.

"Tea time" said Thomas with a laugh and he rubbed his tummy.

As he followed the children into the kitchen Dreenee thought to himself that Time would have to wait, for he was very hungry. On the table was a lot of bread and butter and jam, and milk — and he knew all the new names. Jam he really loved. It tasted like the honey his People collected.

After the meal he had to wash his hands and face, which was a strange new thing, but he copied Thomas and Alice. Next he watched the children clean their teeth with a brush. He was handed a little brush but he threw it away. Spitting was nice, but he did not like brushing; and he did not like it when the woman laughed at him!

"Time for bed", said the man.

That word again!

"Time? Time?" said Dreenee, looking straight at the man, with the question in his eyes.

"Clock", said Thomas, and the big man put his hand in one of his pockets and pulled out a very small clock. It was much smaller than the one on the mantelpiece. Dreenee was fascinated and he was even allowed to hold it. "Time?" he said, and everyone nodded. He put it to his ears to listen and turned it over to look all round it. Vaguely he realised that Clock and Time were much the same thing. Somehow, he thought, he must take Time back to Ningermaner. But how? He would need to be very cunning to make them forget he was still holding Time in his hands.

He thought very hard. Then, suddenly he started to carol loudly, and slipped Time into his pocket.

Alice and Thomas, and even the man and the woman, were amazed to hear Dreenee carol just like a magpie. Everyone stared at him and said "More, more!"

They all tried to imitate Dreenee but the noises that came out made him laugh. Again and again Thomas tried. Soon everyone was laughing. Dreenee smiled to himself as he felt Time in his pocket. Even Ningermaner would be proud of his cunning ways!

He gave them the call of the black cockatoo, then the high-pitched whine of the tiger-wolf and, last of all, the softer thin piping trill of the robin redbreast. And still they said "More, more!"

But at last Dreenee could go on no longer so the man took him by the hand and led him over to the sleeping hut.

"Time for bed, Dreenee", he said, and patted him on the head. Then he lit the fire using the two flints and went out, locking the door behind him.

As Dreenee listened to the white man lock the door he took Time out of his pocket to have a quick look, thinking pockets really were a very good idea.

14. Up the Smoke Hole

As soon as he was alone, Dreenee took the can of water and put the fire out. He peered through the bars on the window. Sun was starting to walk down behind his hills and there under the yellow gums a flock of magpies strutted about.

Dreenee knew he could not get back to camp before Sun went away, but he did not intend to spend all night in this dark room. He looked up the smoke hole again, and quickly filled his pockets with interesting things.

There were so many things he wanted to take; yet he would need two hands to climb up the smoke-hole. He looked longingly at a pot. It was so big and he needed to use both his hands. Supposing he put it upside down on his head! He simply must take it back to the women and show them how to boil eggs. And he must take the sheepskin.

Stooping, he wriggled inside the fireplace. His fingers holding on to the rough stones, and the pot upside down on his head, he scrambled up, the rolled-up sheepskin under one arm. Soon he was lying flat on the wooden roof, his heart pounding as he looked about from under the rim of the pot.

Dog had started to bark furiously. He must hurry!

There under the trees his magpies were watching him. Softly they warbled while he slithered down the roof and dropped lightly into a bush. Then all together they flew down the gully, singing their urgent Travel Song.

Dreenee ran fast like an emu, leaping over logs and crashing down into the gully, until the house was out of sight. Sun was sinking fast, but he knew he could not race Sun. The pot was quite heavy, so sometimes he carried it in one hand and sometimes in the other.

His head was almost aching with so much New Knowledge but he knew he must tell the People about Pungertenner and the magic thing that made fire, and show them Time. They were the three most important things.

Soon the trees became mere shadows as the twilight deepened, but still the magpies flew, always carolling to him and always just in front.

Making his way over several hills and gullies he at last came to the Fat Doe River. Here it was quite dark and nearby he heard the long drawn-out rasping screech of the masked owl. Trembling with fear of the Raegeowropper, the Evil Spirit which dwelt in dark places, he waded through the water and scrambled up the muddy bank. The pot weighed him down and his wet trousers clung to his legs like slimy seaweed, but he managed to keep the sheepskin dry.

Here, on the top of the bank, his magpies were waiting for him and in the distance he could see the light of his People's campfires. He flopped down among them in the long grass, glad to be through the terrifying dark wet place. The owl continued its monotonous lonely call and all about frogs croaked. Possums screeched and fought in the trees, and far away Dreenee could hear the whine of a tiger-wolf. He kept his gaze on the bright eyes of his magpies and closed his mind to the sounds of the bush. His legs trembled and his arms ached from the weight of Pot; but the worst part was over. He was through the dark wet place and Moon had begun to climb, flooding the Land with a soft silver light. Now he must sit and plan what he would say and do.

He knew that the women would be angry. Maybe his hair would be pulled again and, worse still, maybe they would put him in a tree and jeer at him. But no matter what they did, he must show them Pot and give them his New Knowledge of cooking eggs in water.

Dreenee looked again at his clothes. He really liked the bright shirt which was the colour of Sky and, although the trousers were scratchy things, uncomfortable when wet, making running difficult, he liked the pockets. So many things could be collected in pockets, but he knew he would not walk into camp wearing clothes.

He emptied his pockets out and looked carefully at all his

possessions. As he did so, his magpies moved closer and formed a black and white chortling circle around him. He produced a shiny little knife, a nail, a long piece of cord and, last of all, Time carefully wrapped in Hanky from one pocket. He placed them on the sheepskin, watching the eyes of his magpies shine red in the light of Moon.

"Wait till you see what I have in the other pocket", he laughed. And then he pulled out one carrot and a few of the white man's seeds. (Actually he had two carrots in that pocket, and a fistful of the seeds, but these he was determined to keep for Ningermaner.)

Dreenee was hungry now Moon was up and the camp only a short walk away, so he took one big bite of the carrot and bit off a small portion for each bird. They obviously were delighted with the new taste, for their eyes shone even brighter. Then he gave each one a round yellow seed and crunched up a few himself. He could think best of all when he was chewing, and he had a big decision to make about his possessions.

He picked up Time wrapped in Hanky and much to his surprise the old leader came forward, took Hanky in his beak and put it on the ground. Then he turned Time over in Dreenee's hand, with such a quaint expression of curiosity on his face that the youngster burst out laughing.

"Come on, maggy magpies", he chuckled. "You are the clever ones who were chosen to push up Sky in the Dark Waiting Time, and to bring Sun to shine on Land. What shall I do with these things?"

A wombat waddled quite close, then seeing the boy and the magpies it lumbered away with a startled grunt, but Dreenee did not even see or hear it, so intent was he. The magpies were very close and he could almost hear them thinking and planning.

A moment later the leader stepped forward and, picking up Hanky in his beak, silently rose and flew about a stone's throw away to a rocky place beside the dark river. The other birds followed him, chortling their urgent Travel

Song. But Dreenee did not follow them. He was afraid of the dark place.

Presently they returned.

"So you want me to put my things in that dark place, do you? . . . But what if Evil Spirits lurk there?"

Silently the magpies moved closer and stared at him and Dreenee could almost feel them soak up his fear and take it away.

Before he fully realised what he was doing he stood up, brave and strong, and took off his shirt and trousers. Next he stuffed the cord and knife in one pocket, and then he took the second carrot out of the other pocket and tucked it quickly into his mop of tight curly hair for Ningermaner. Last of all he put Time very carefully in the pocket with two golden seeds. He then rolled the shirt and trousers up in the sheepskin. Leaving Pot behind, he followed the birds over to the dark place. He saw his white Hanky in a shaft of Moonlight at the entrance to a small dark cave. Quickly he picked up Hanky and tucked it into his bundle and placed everything in the dark hole.

He heard the nervous spitting sound of the masked owl, then out flew several black bats, but already Dreenee was racing back through shadows to the silver light of Moon. He picked up Pot, and on fast feet, with no trousers to tangle about his legs, he sped towards the camp of his People.

15. New Knowledge for Ningermaner

Moonah was feeding her new baby when Dreenee walked into camp carrying Pot. Relief and anger welled in her as she saw her son. For two days the People had been searching for him.

She rushed over to him and all the women and children

followed. Everyone seemed to be yelling at once as Dreenee tried to tell them of the white man on Horse who had snatched him up and taken him to his house and locked him up. Tears rolled down his cheeks as he tried to explain, but it was no good. No-one would listen to him. He only knew he was too tired for words.

He felt Ningermaner's arms lift him up and carry him away.

"Was it the magpies again?" she asked, and all he could do was nod. Suddenly he couldn't speak any more. He just wanted to soak up the gentle warmth of Ningermaner and let her rock out his pain.

Through half-closed eyes he watched the other women looking at Pot and all talking excitedly together. He saw the stern eyes of the men watching the women from their sleeping places. Then he saw his mother take Pot down to the river and throw it into a deep hole.

Two tears overflowed and the small boy began to sob until sleep came softly and he felt himself sinking down into a deep dark place beside Pot.

Carrying Dreenee over to her own sleeping place, Ningermaner sat down and gazed into the flickering flames of her campfire. Fondly crooning to him and stroking him, she thought about his new smell. Even his skin looked and felt different. It was much paler and it did not feel greasy. She must do something about his skin fast! Already she could see Moonah throw Pot away and it was quite probable she and her friends would soon hurry over to her son. Quickly Ningermaner put a holding spell around Moonah. Moments later she smiled to herself, as Moonah lost her footing and slipped down the muddy bank of the Fat Doe River! Soon Manganinnie and Longameena were helping Moonah, wet and muddy, up the bank and over to their big fire. Children were laughing and rushing about. Only Dreenee lay limp and silent, asleep in her arms.

"Thank you, Old Ones", she smiled. "I see you still know how to amuse yourselves around your campfires in the sky!"

Ningermaner pensively poked the fire and, raking some warm ashes towards her, gently rubbed them into Dreenee's skin. Next she picked up the remains of a snake she had killed the day before and smeared the fatty meat all over him until he smelt nice again. He shone like the wet trunk of a black wattle tree.

Sometimes Dreenee twitched as he slept and Ningermaner knew instinctively that he had had some awful experience, so she croaked a soft healing song as her gentle hands fondled and stroked him.

Suddenly, while she was rubbing her greasy hands through his woolly curls, she felt something new! Cunningly the old woman looked to the place where the women were crowding around Moonah. Then she looked beyond them to where the men were working on their spears and talking earnestly. All was well.

She removed the new thing from Dreenee's hair and smelt and felt it. It looked rather like the pale little roots which grew in the marshes nearby, but it was much bigger and the colour of ochre; she was sure it had not grown in the bush.

She knew she really should keep this new food safely hidden under her kangaroo skin until tomorrow, for it belonged to New Knowledge and must be shared; but somehow the nice smell of it was too much. She took one bite and then another one. Soon Dreenee's carrot was gone.

Afterwards, gazing into the fire, Ningermaner realised that she was beginning to change. Like Dreenee, she was starting to break some of the laws. This New Knowledge should have been shared with the others. She had indeed become an outlaw herself and felt ashamed.

Fire hissed and spat, then suddenly in the flames the gentle smiling face of her husband, the old Leader, came to her. Gazing at her intently, he spoke:

For two days I have walked in the shadow of Dreenee, taking him to New Knowledge, but the People are not yet ready to learn from the pale-faced ones. Mannerganner is young yet and does not fully understand the danger to the People. Learn their ways.

Ningermaner sat quietly thinking for a long time after her husband's face had faded away. Tomorrow she would take Dreenee digging for native bread. Too often he slipped away by himself instead of going food-gathering with the women and young boys and girls. Perhaps when they were alone they could talk about his New Knowledge, and then they would share it with Mannerganner. It must be important. It certainly sounded exciting. It should be shared, for this was the Law.

16. That Other World

"I wonder if Dreenee has brothers and sisters?" Alice asked her mother when she was being tucked into bed.

"He probably has, dear," Lizzie said. "The natives usually have lots and lots of children."

"Well, won't they miss him, Mama? I would miss Thomas if he disappeared. Won't they come looking for him?" Alice persisted.

"I hope not, for our sakes," said Lizzie thoughtfully.

"I like Dreenee. Couldn't he sleep in our room?" Alice asked. "He must feel lonely all by himself in the storeroom."

"I know, dear," Lizzie said, concern showing in her eyes. "Not tonight. I will ask your father what he thinks. Now snuggle down. It is well past your bedtime."

"Could I go and sleep with Dreenee?" Thomas asked.

"No, Thomas. Blow out the candle and get some sleep. It's been an exciting day for everyone."

"Dreenee's fun!" Thomas said. "He doesn't miss a trick. He never stops looking and listening, and wanting to learn more words. I think he's really clever. I wonder how old he is? He is as tall as me . . . Do you think he is seven too, Mama?"

"Probably, Thomas. Now blow out your candle at once and we'll talk about it in the morning."

Edward was gazing pensively into the fire when Lizzie settled herself into her chair. She wanted time to think. Even last night she had thought it was rather rash of Edward to have captured Dreenee. Hadn't Robert Knopwood stressed the fact that the Aborigines would keep out of the way if the settlers didn't interfere with them? Lizzie tried to console herself with the knowledge that other settlers had done the very same thing. Even the Governor had been given a black child. But to Lizzie it didn't seem right. She knew she was only making excuses for Edward. Today she had begun to see Dreenee, not as a toy to pick up and play with, but as a very intelligent and brave young boy. How, she wondered, would Thomas cope if he were captured by the natives? And how was Dreenee's mother feeling at this very moment?

Her eyes moved from her patchwork quilt to her husband's face. Lizzie could almost think his thoughts. He, too, was wondering what was the right thing to do. He turned to Lizzie and looked at her with real confusion and remorse in his eyes.

"Lizzie, my love, what can we do? It was foolhardy of me to grab the child. If only I had stopped to think! I am little better than a bushranger!"

Edward poked the fire with such vigour that it sparked and flared.

"Come, my dear, you mustn't reproach yourself. I was quite enchanted when you rode into the yard with him! Blaming ourselves is not the answer." "I didn't think of him as a person, Lizzie. Rather as something interesting to bring home from the bush. We have seen so little of the natives really, only the smoke from their campfires at this time of the year as they move down from the Highlands to the sea. They probably know more about us than we do of them. They could so easily have burnt us out, or speared

70

our sheep, but we have been lucky . . . Until now we have done nothing to offend them. Now look what I've done! At this very moment they could be planning revenge, and I must admit they would be justified. Drat it, Lizzie! We have come halfway round the world to start a new life. Right from the beginning we were aware of the dangers and hardships. I'm blessed if I'll let my stupidity endanger my family, and undo all we have worked so hard to accomplish. We must get Dreenee back to his own people as quickly as possible — but how?"

Together they talked, and eventually they decided the safest way was for Edward to ride out at daybreak and look for signs of smoke, and then to return for Dreenee. It would be far too dangerous to ride into camp with him, and it would be inhumane simply to leave him in the bush. He would leave the youngster near enough to the camp to find his own way. Their only concern was that the natives might have already moved on, but they would face that later, if necessary.

Edward was lucky. Riding fast in the dawn light he found smoke in a gully about three miles away, and within the hour he was home again. He barely had time to swing out of the saddle when Thomas came hurtling through the gate, with Alice close behind him.

"Papa! Dreenee's gone! What will we do?"

"Yes, Papa, what will we do? Please find him for me!" Alice begged.

"One minute, children. How do you know? Tell me exactly what happened, son."

"I woke up early wondering about Dreenee, so I went over to the storeroom and looked in at the window. I couldn't see him inside, but I noticed footprints in Mama's garden, so I told her. We all looked, and Maria could follow his tracks right down to the creek. She was better than us, Papa, and she's very upset," said Thomas. "Mama is with her now."

"Yes, Papa, Maria was crying," Alice confirmed, with tears in her own eyes.

"However did he get out, Thomas? I locked the door myself. Did he break the window?"

"No, Papa. Maria thinks he climbed up the chimney last night, before the frost," Thomas replied.

"The chimney!" Edward exclaimed, relief welling up inside him. "Put Ginger in the loose-box, children, while I get some breakfast," he said as he handed the reins to Thomas.

Moments later Lizzie came running towards him. She swung her arms around her husband's neck and together they laughed, freed from the strain of indecision.

"The clever young rascal!" Edward chuckled. "He has outwitted us all. Who would have thought of climbing up the chimney?"

"I must make a sketch of the shed with Dreenee coming out of the chimney. It will amuse our folk at home," Lizzie giggled.

"I hope the kettle is on, my love. We are not out of the woods yet. I won't be at rest until the natives move on."

"I think we will have to watch Maria, Edward. She is very tearful and restless. We must keep her busy and try to include her in our conversations more than we have done in the past. She must feel dreadfully lonely at times."

"Do you know, Lizzie, I didn't even see Dreenee's tracks near the muddy creek, but I believe Maria did. It will make her feel more important. Was she the first one to realise about the chimney?"

"Yes, Edward. She thinks he put the fire out straight away and left before it was dark."

"There's no doubt about Dreenee!" Edward laughed. "He has outwitted us all! I suppose my precious pocket watch went up the chimney with him? I've missed it and I remember his fascination with it . . . They say the natives have no real concept of time — not as we know it, anyway. We can't even find time to have a leisurely ramble in the bush. We are endlessly racing against time: time to fence and cultivate new land; time to split more shingles. We are always wishing there were more hours in the day, always racing the clock."

Edward paused, and then he laughed. "Oh, well, if the young scallywag has taken time with him and I've lost track of it, time doesn't really matter! Without time on my hands I may as well change my mind about getting the autumn turnips in, and simply laze about on the roof looking for signs of smoke or approaching visitors!" Edward laughed but he glanced at the clock as he hurried out of the kitchen.

17. The Secret of Pot

Children scampered about throwing stones into tussocks and sedges and occasionally a startled native hen fled before them, giving away the secret of her nest of eggs. Now and then a woman would stop to collect seeds.

Ningermaner made sure that no-one saw her as she made her way back to camp and the place where the new thing lay deep in the river. The women, she knew, would be busy for most of the day and she could see by the fire the men were lighting that they were hunting in the hills. The river was muddy but not deep here, so it should not be too hard to find the pot.

Passing under the stringybark, the old woman called to Dreenee and hurried along, thinking about diving, for she had not dived deep for some time. It would not be deep and dangerous like diving for crayfish in Sea. The Fat Doe River flowed quietly through the marshes here. It was quite shallow and muddy in the summertime.

Disappearing underwater, the old woman groped in the mud for Dreenee's Pot. Twice she came up for air, as Dreenee watched. Then she came up with Pot.

Dreenee let out a loud "Wah!" of delight as he saw his

73

precious Pot. Leaping in the air he laughed aloud, and rolled over laughing.

"Pot, Pot!", he said, using the new word for Ningermaner to learn. Proudly he filled it with water and carried it to the fire.

The young boy and his grandmother sat silently watching as the water heated. In a little while Dreenee started to talk about all the things he had seen put in the pots for cooking. He talked about eggs and carrots, potatoes and meat. Once he had started talking, all his New Knowledge tumbled out. He chattered non-stop like a gurgling creek about Cow, Sheep, Horse and Dog; about Pungertenner and Time, about Alice and Thomas, about the man and the woman; and about the smoke-hole. Last of all he told Ningermaner about the sheepskin and his other possessions in the little cave.

It was warm beside the fire, yet a cold shiver ran through Ningermaner as she listened to Dreenee. So much New Knowledge! It was no wonder that he had needed to rush about today, throwing stones and climbing trees! It was far too much New Knowledge for any young boy to handle alone.

The water boiled over while Dreenee talked, making fire hiss. Ashes rose in the still air and fluttered down like pale feathers, to settle in their hair.

At last Dreenee ran out of talk. He slipped away among the bullrushes to collect the eggs of a duck whose nest he had seen from a stringybark tree. He came back with four eggs and Ningermaner watched as he proudly dropped them gently into Pot and gave her the white man's word, 'Egg'.

While they waited for the eggs to cook, Ningermaner closed her mind to everything around her. She had several big decisions to make, and although she didn't want Dreenee tormented or disappointed, she knew that all this New Knowledge simply must be shared with the People. Mannerganner, she knew, could punish Dreenee for taking things away from the white man's settlement and also for hiding them in the cave instead of bringing them straight to him. He was very young to be the new leader. How she wished her wise old husband was still Chief of the Big River tribe! Wistfully Ningermaner gazed into the fire and moments later Warrabee seemed to be talking to her:

Learn from Dreenee about cooking in water and keep with him the secret of the pot. It will not matter if the pot lies hidden in the river for one full cycle but it is very important that you go to the cave with him. Let him show his possessions to you and talk as much as he needs, for he has done well to collect so much New Knowledge. Hide all tracks near the cave and roll the possessions up in the sheepskin. Then take them straight to Mannerganner. You will find him waiting for you outside the camp.

Fear not for Dreenee because I will be there. I will put wise words in Mannerganner's mouth and the right decisions in his head. Go now and enjoy the eggs with Dreenee.

After Warrabee's voice had faded away, Ningermaner reached for her kangaroo skin. Sun was warm, yet she felt cold. Her knees shook as excitement mingled with fear. None of her People liked change, but now they were having to share part of their tribal land with these Intruders, and their new animals.

Dreenee's eyes never left his grandmother's face as they each ate two eggs.

"Thank you, Dreenee. Eggs are soft and warm. I like them. I think Pot could do many things. Eels would be nice cooked in hot water and so would lizards and echidna", she said.

"And sheep, Ningermaner. Wait until you taste that meat", Dreenee said.

Together they sat thinking of Pot and food. Dreenee swelled with pride to hear her praise and see the smile on her face. Praise from Ningermaner was wonderful. So was simply sitting close to her and soaking up her thoughts about Pot. She would not make him return Pot to its owners, nor show it to the People today, he knew, for she had left her mind wide open to him.

Manfully Dreenee stood up, straight and tall as a blue-gum sapling, and picked up Pot.

"I will put Pot back in the river", he told his grandmother. "That is the best, while we decide what to do with the things in the little cave."

"Good", said Ningermaner, with a rather cunning smile.

Dreenee carried Pot a stone's throw upstream from the big hole, and here let it slide into the shallow mud.

18. Sharing New Knowledge

Sun shone warm as feathers on their backs as the couple sat outside the cave and Dreenee proudly unrolled the sheepskin.

Wisely Ningermaner sat without speaking, knowing it was now her time to look and listen. She watched as he put on the shirt and trousers and showed her the pockets. He came close to her, wound the pocket watch as Alice's father had done, and asked if she could hear something ticking like a beetle. Carefully he gave it to her, together with the word Time.

Ningermaner was fascinated. "Time?", she said, as she turned it over in her hands. "What is Time? How do the white people use Time?"

Proudly Dreenee showed her how the two hands moved, rather like Sun across Sky and even as she watched, Ningermaner could see the big hand moving very slowly like Sun.

"Time is very important to white man; he carries it about in his pocket", said Dreenee showing her the trouser pockets. "I think we should show this one to Mannerganner," replied Ningermaner.

Ningermaner was surprised with her own words and even more surprised when Dreenee nodded his head. She had expected Dreenee to beg to keep Time for himself, but instead he put it back in the pocket and began to take off the clothes.

"I have some seeds in the other pocket. I would like to keep some of them", he said, "for they taste good, but I think I should show the other things to Mannerganner. Do you think he will be angry with me? Will you come and help me?"

Ningermaner hugged her grandson. "No, Dreenee. Your help-spirits will give you the right words, and maybe they will even put a holding spell around Mannerganner's decisions and help him decide what to do with the clothes and the sheepskin and Time."

They decided to keep Pot in the river, and Hanky and the seeds in the cave for one whole cycle. "They will be our very own secret. Go now and climb a tree to keep watch, while I roll up the clothes in the sheepskin and put Hanky and the seeds inside the cave."

With great pride Ningermaner watched the boy bound away and scramble up into the spreading arms of a stringybark gum. She wanted to look very carefully at everything, especially the sheepskin. So after she had put Hanky away with some of the seeds, and scattered some twigs and mouldy leaves about to hide their tracks, she picked up the clothes and the sheep-skin and walked downstream, away from the cave. Here she settled down to feel and smell the new skin, and have one last look at Time before she put it back in the pocket. As she did so a few seeds fell out, so she scratched some earth over them to hide them.

A flock of magpies circled overhead and settled in a nearby tree. Soon Dreenee was warbling sweetly with them. Peal after peal of rich melodious magpie song filled the gully, taking away Dreenee's worries about the new people and all their possessions.

Sitting in his tree he could see with his inside eye what Ningermaner was now doing. She was hiding the seeds, planting them like the white man did. He smiled to himself. Ningermaner, he knew, was breaking the Law, but he would let her have her secret. In his hair he had his own secret. It was the nail which Alice's father had given him. Ningermaner had found the carrot, but the nail he would share with Lugga.

He swung himself lightly down from the tree. The magpies rose in the air and flew up and away over the wattle trees. Watching them follow the river downstream towards camp and listening to their urgent Travel Song, Dreenee knew he must follow them and share the new knowledge with Mannerganner.

"Come, Ningermaner", he called. "We must go."

Mannerganner was restless. Soon he must call the People together and leave on the longest journey of the food-gathering ritual, a migration which would take them to the Seafood Land. Nearly every day scouts returned to camp with more news of the Intruders. There was no longer only one settlement on the banks of the Wide River. Farms were now springing up like mushrooms, all the way down to the place where the first sailing ship had come in and not gone away, four cycles ago.

Wanting to think, he walked upstream and sat on a log. Moments later Ningermaner and Dreenee appeared. They were walking towards him and the young boy was carrying a strange object. Ningermaner spoke first:

"We wish to sit in council with you, Mannerganner, for Dreenee has some important news to share with you. When he escaped from the settlement yesterday he brought with him some of white man's possessions, but instead of coming straight to you he hid them in a cave because he knew his mother would not understand."

Ningermaner sat down on the grass, her eyes never leaving her Leader's face, while Dreenee placed the bundle on the grass between them. Mannerganner felt angry words coming. He was about to say that Dreenee must be put in a tree and jeered at tonight because he had left camp alone and had not shared Common Knowledge, when suddenly he felt wise words in his head.

"Show me what you have in the bundle, and then I want you to tell me about everything you saw and heard at the white man's camp."

It was easy after that. Dreenee showed his Leader the sheepskin and the clothes, and put Time in his hands. Then he talked non-stop about the ways of the white ones and about Pungertenner. Last of all he told Mannerganner how he had escaped up the smoke hole. Mannerganner sat quietly listening while he watched the big hand of Time moving.

"We want nothing to do with these possessions", he said, "but it is good to know about them. Go now Dreenee, and tell Meenapeekameena to gather together the other councillors and come to me. You and Ningermaner may sit in council with us."

After Mannerganner had spoken he wondered why he had made such a decision. Women and children were never included in such matters. Then as he silently turned Time over in his hands, he realised that the old ways of the People were not always suited to these big, new problems. It wasn't easy to share tribal lands with strangers and their new animals, but in order to survive his People must try to understand the strange ways of the white people. Mannerganner told Dreenee to place all the possessions, except for Time, in a nearby hollow tree. Here they would stay until his people returned again. Meanwhile he would decide what to do with them.

The men wanted to know more and more about the magic stick which had killed the two swans, and also the stones which made fire, so Dreenee was often invited to sit in council with them and nearly every night a new story was added to the old songs and dances. Sometimes it was about one of the new animals and at other times the women wanted to know about milking and sewing and cooking sheep meat in pots of hot water. The women always laughed loudest about the peculiar custom of catching water from the roof and carrying it inside their homes in containers, when there was plenty of water in the river only a stone's throw away.

"Are you sure about that one, Dreenee?" his mother asked him.

So one day he and Lugga made a special gutter out of a thick piece of bark, and tied it on to Moonah's family shelter with string they made by twisting strands of a reed. But the rain water ran down the gutter and into her little shelter.

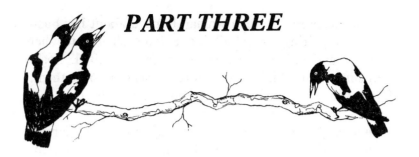

PART THREE

19. Return to the Fat Doe

As Dreenee travelled with his People over to the Seafood Land and then on up to the Land of Many Lakes and beyond to the Lake of Dreams, scarcely a day went by when he did not think about his beautiful Pot lying in the bottom of the river, but the novelty of the pocket watch was soon forgotten. Time seemed to have no real meaning, so Dreenee put it in Ningermaner's basket thinking that one day he might return it to the settlement.

As summer began to fade, and the food gathering cycle called the People back to the Fat Doe River again, Dreenee thought more and more about Pot, the possessions, little Alice and the beautiful Horse. Some nights his dreams were full of Horse.

How he longed to climb on Horse and race away faster than the kangaroo! He had so many beautiful places to show Horse. Perhaps they could learn to exchange New Knowledge. Horse might even be able to tell him what it was like over the rim of the sea. Perhaps one day Horse might even travel with him to visit the tribes at the top of Droemerdeene's Land?

A highland mist hung low over the Fat Doe River when Dreenee and his family eventually reached the campsite nearest to Pot.

All day Rain had fallen in cold wet sheets. Now Sun was trying to shine through a heavy blanket of cloud. Tonight would be cold. Wind and Rain had weathered the campsite, making it clean again, but they had also flattened some of the bark shelters. So each woman hurried about her business of repairing or rebuilding a bark shelter for her husband and children, while her husband waited. Some men simply sat while the wind-break was built over them. There was plenty of food in a pile beside the cold wet hearths, so they rested, awaiting the meal.

Dreenee and his friends frolicked among the huge rain-washed gums as they collected long strips of bark for patching some of the shelters. While they worked, the young boy remembered the big man at the settlement and his nails. It would be interesting to see if his huts had been battered and tossed by Wind and Rain, or flattened by the weight of Snow. Nails, he thought, might be a very good idea.

As soon as he had checked on his Pot he would slip away for a whole day's looking and listening at the settlement.

His eyes became mere slits as he worked, planning the next few days. He didn't see Mannerganner approach and his voice startled him:

"Dreenee, go to the hollow tree where we hid the sheep-skin bundle when last we camped here. Bring it to me."

Dreenee walked a short distance, his heart pounding with pride and anticipation. Before he reached the tree he knew what had taken place at a glance. Sheep's wool, matted and stained, lay strewn on the damp ground. The shirt and trousers had been dragged out too, where rain and sun had bleached and rotted them. Dreenee smelt devil in the pungent hollow where the distinctive droppings of matted hair and bone were scattered. He searched for, and found, the knife and the piece of cord. With these he ran back to the camp and sat in front of Mannerganner who listened, gazing all the while into the embers. When Dreenee finished, the Leader spoke without emotion:

"It is good; we have no use for white man's skins . . . show me how you saw the white man use this knife Dreenee. I wish to carry it with my spears . . .'

A little way off Ningermanner too had been recalling all that had taken place on their last visit. She would slip away and see what had happened to her seeds. Just in case she needed it, she would take a grinding stone and a firestick. Bread made from sag corn was tasty. These new seeds might also grind well and, mixed with water and cooked on Fire, they might taste just as good, or even better.

Then of course there was Pot. If the eggs could be cooked in water, perhaps eel could be too, or even echidna. Maybe some of the tubers and yams and yabbies also, but first she wanted to find out for herself. The People did not like Change, so any change must be carefully planned before she shared it, according to the Law.

Smiling to herself Ningermaner walked to the place where she had planted the white man's seeds. All she found there were a few round wallaby droppings scattered upon the bare, scratched earth.

20. The Five Intruders

Dreenee stretched his long lean limbs and looked about. It was good to be back in the gully of his birth. He felt a kinship here beside the Fat Doe River which was stronger than in any other campsite. Dawn was breaking in long soft folds of light and, as always, he was hungry. His first thoughts were for the manna tree.

Stealthily the young boy slipped away from camp on silent toes. Soon he was speeding beneath the tall grey, shadowy gums and feeling the wonder of the dawning day.

Possums scurried up trees as he ran and a devil, well-fed and sleepy, watched him furtively from behind a blackened stump. Here and there kangaroos loped about in lazy leaps or stopped, crouching, to nibble the dew-fresh grasses. But Dreenee was only interested in reaching the manna gum.

Arriving in a sheltered gully Dreenee found his favourite tree well laden with the sweet food. The ants had already arrived, but there was plenty for him too. Contentedly he squatted down and feasted on the white crumbs which had dropped from the under surfaces of the leaves, while a noisy flock of parakeets watched him from a nearby honeysuckle tree. When he had eaten enough he followed a small creek back to the river, looking and listening for signs of nesting birds. One tawny breast feather poised like a butterfly on a tall reed caught his attention and moments later he found a soft pile of feathers. Dreenee's eyes shone! The nest was deserted and beautifully concealed from the bigger birds of prey. In no time he was sucking furiously on the tasty warm food and drilling a hole in another egg. Already Sun was peeping down into the gully, so he hurriedly ate two more eggs, then ran down alongside the river until he could see into camp. All was quiet. No-one stirred and Dreenee chuckled, feeling pleased with himself as he chewed on a peppermint leaf. No-one need know about the manna or the eggs. He would wash and drink in the river, then he would be practising stone-throwing or simply looking and listening. The leaf of the peppermint tree was certainly a clever idea for concealing the smell of food.

Dreenee loved this time of day when there was no-one about. There was so much to see and hear when Sun first shone on the Land. It was a busy time when the night creatures were returning to their sleeping places and the day creatures were just waking up; and best of all he loved to hear the sunrise song of the magpies.

Standing quietly beside the river, Dreenee listened for magpies and watched as shafts of light drifted across the Land and touched the water. This was the time of day when his shadow was long, so he stood watching it grow long and strong. Soon he would be a big warrior like his father, he thought to himself. Today it was the longest he had ever seen, so he laughed aloud and jumped down the bank to drink and wash away any tell-tale signs of food on his face and hands. He sucked up the cool fresh water, then lay down on the bank, watching his own reflection. Presently there was a swirl in the water in front of him, and then another one. Coarse brown fur humped out of the water and Dreenee watched as *oonah* the platypus played. Soon there were two of them frolicking and twisting together, sometimes floating quietly and sometimes darting about, leaving a silver trail behind them as their broad flat bills cut the surface of the water.

Many small birds came to drink as Dreenee looked and listened, so he kept very still, just as he had been taught. He could hear the high-pitched trill of the blue wren, and he mimicked the sound. Moments later the bird appeared and flitted from twig to twig, coming closer and looking comically confused until its mate arrived. Then together they drank and splashed about.

Another deeper chattering trill next attracted Dreenee's attention and while he listened a scarlet robin landed on a stump, only to flutter away when an old wombat shuffled too close to him, looking tired and sleepy. Dreenee's attention focused now on the wombat and he noticed that he had been in a fight. His nose was bleeding and he waddled along with quite a limp. Watching him, Dreenee threw a small pebble at him. Wombat grunted and, breaking into a startled clumsy canter, lumbered down the bank and disappeared, while the little blue wrens flew away, trilling an urgent warning of danger.

Listening to the bird calls and watching across the river, the youngster waited, expecting to see the old wombat appear on the other side when, much to his surprise, he saw smoke curling in the still air. Smoke! There should be no smoke, except at the People's camp. This hunting ground belonged to his People of the Big River tribe and that was a sacred place which belonged only to the older men!

Dreenee's head was in a whirl. Quickly he flattened himself in the silver tussocks and began to chew on a pithy reed while he decided what to do. Curiosity mingled with his original dismay while he pondered. Should he return to camp and tell the People? Or should he look and listen longer? He closed his mind to everything else except the smoke and willed his magpies to come and help him.

Moments later he heard them calling loudly as they followed the river, coming closer! Dreenee was delighted with himself; his magic powers were certainly getting stronger! Even as he waited, they fluttered down beside him in the long grass and, forming a circle round him, they stared at him until he found he couldn't look away.

Moments later the big birds rose in the air and flew off in the direction of the smoke and Dreenee followed them. Over the river and through the trees they travelled until the magpies landed and concealed themselves in some tussocks. Only a stone's throw away the young boy could see a strange shelter. It was bigger than the People's simple bark shelters and was made of stuff like cloth that he had seen at Alice's home. It was held up by something like a climbing rope stretched between two trees. He remembered hearing the men talk about such shelters called 'tents'. Near the shelter were the scattered ashes of a fire from which the smoke curled, and here several pots were turned upside-down. Seeing the pots, Dreenee became excited.

"So you want me to take another pot back to camp, do you?", he whispered to the leader, but to his surprise the old bird stepped forward with a very stern look in his eyes and Dreenee knew it was something else, so he settled down to wait.

Moments later a pale-faced man came out of the shelter. His body and feet were covered with clothes and in one hand he carried a shiny stick. It was the same as the one Dreenee had seen Alice's father carry inside after killing the swans!

The youngsters eyes were wide with fear. He glanced at his magpies. They stared hard at him and made a muffled chortle no louder than a whisper. Slowly he felt their thoughts come inside his head, and his body trembled.

"So you want me to grab the magic stick, do you?" he whispered. "Tell me when."

While Dreenee watched, the man picked up a pot in the other hand and, looking about him, began to walk towards the river. Suddenly he stopped and, dropping the pot, raised the metal stick to his shoulder and pointed it in the direction of a mob of kangaroos quietly grazing in the next gully downstream. A moment later there was a terrible booming noise, louder than thunder, louder than anything Dreenee had ever heard. A fat young doe fell to the ground, while the other kangaroos bounded away.

Dreenee blinked his eyes and looked again. His legs were shaking! The man had killed a kangaroo, yet it was at least three stone's throws away!

He glanced at his magpies. They flattened themselves in the tussocks around him, so he slid in among them, flat on the ground, and divided his attention between the white man and the tent. The man hurried away towards the dead doe and bending over it seemed to be gutting it. Noises came from the tent. Next, two other men appeared. Soon they were stretching themselves and looking over towards the place where the kangaroo lay.

"Well done, Laycock!" one of them called, and the man busy beside the doe turned and waved to them.

Dreenee remembered 'Well done'. Alice's mother and father had used the words several times. But 'Laycock' he did not know. Perhaps it was the name of the man?

This man now moved towards the river, carrying the kangaroo and the dreadful booming stick. Around the shelter there were now four men moving about near the fire.

Four men! Dreenee was terrified! Perhaps he should run home to his family. Five Intruders were far too much for any boy to cope with. This was now a matter for the warriors. He tried to get up and run, but his body wouldn't move. The magpies wanted him to stay and there was nothing he could do about it. Their will was stronger than his own, so he settled down to look and listen with the birds.

Laycock had now reached the river a few stones' throws away, further downstream. He put the kangaroo down and propped his shiny stick against a tree. Next he removed all his clothes and waded into the water. What a pale skin the man had! Even his toes were almost the colour of snow. Dreenee was fascinated. He watched the man swim slowly down along the river, leaving behind him a huge pile of clothes. Perhaps he should grab them? Then the man couldn't walk far (especially without his shoes). So intent was Dreenee that he almost forgot about his magpies so, when the old leader pecked him gently on the leg, the young boy was startled. He looked towards the shelter and saw the four men walking away in the other direction. Now and then they bent down, as if collecting eggs or tubers.

"Now, Dreenee — now", said the magpies, all together. The four men were still moving about among the sedges; Laycock was still swimming and splashing about. Dreenee darted forward and grabbed the magic stick and carrying it very carefully, dashed back to the camp of his People.

The women were already moving about when Dreenee sat down beside the fire. Gasping for breath, he told them about the Intruders and held up the magic stick.

The women all seemed to yell together. The men looked round, all together, wondering what all the fuss was about. Children stared at him through sleepy brown eyes.

Suddenly Moonah grabbed the magic stick from his hand and sped down to the river. Dreenee watched as she hurled it into a deep hole. He heard the splash, and as it sank to the bottom his heart also sank. He crept away before they all started jeering at him and from his hiding place watched as the men and the women argued.

Taking their spears, two men left the camp to follow Dreenee's tracks to the place where he had grabbed the magic stick; he realised that Mannerganner had sent them to watch and listen.

Soon the women and children were busy collecting their things and starting to follow Mannerganner further upstream. When Ningermaner realised that Dreenee was not with them, she searched for his tracks and followed them. The old woman found him sobbing behind a fallen tree.

21. *Leading Away*

Mannerganner's shoulder twitched, pointing the way as he led his People, but it was not a very strong twitch; he was young and sometimes unsure of himself. With a show of great authority he walked fast, his body held straight as a young sapling and his feet stamping hard into the sweet wet earth; feet calling the Good Spirits to walk with them away from the white man's camp and lips mouthing the words of a sacred song.

Above the beating of his heart he heard their footsteps following him. The danger had passed! They would be led to safety.

"Wah! Wah!", he breathed aloud in praise of the Old Ones who had come to walk with his tribe. His deepset eyes shone now where only a moment ago they had shown fear and confusion. He was indeed their Leader! He could call up the Old Ones!

Quietly Mannerganner gave the order to rest, and then he left them, climbing to the top of a hill to look around. Below him he could see his People waiting for him. All was well.

Looking back he could see his two scouts examining the deserted campfire of the Intruders and then, much further away, a wisp of dust and the blurred outline of figures moving across the flat, silver marshes towards the steep gullies which would take them out of the Big River Land. As Mannerganner's eyes became accustomed to the distance he could see specks of colour and clumsy figures carrying heavy burdens. There were five of them.

Why, he wondered, did they carry so many possessions, and why did they wear bright colours? Such colours belonged to the birds and the flowers, not to men. They seemed to have no fear of being seen, and no common sense. They did not keep to the timber, or the high ground.

As the Intruders disappeared down a gully, a sweet song welled deep inside him and flowed out over the ancient Land. Softly he sang to the Old Ones, thanking them for what they had done for his People. Tonight around the campfire he would give a new song to them, but now he must leave his lookabout hill and lead them to a new camping place.

22. *The Longboat*

Twice the food-gathering cycle travelled full circle. Ningermaner sat looking out to sea, watching the waves roll in from over the rim of the world, and beyond the waves to the finger of land where purple mountains climbed out of Sea, and small islands sat like nesting birds in the Bay of Oysters. Letting the sands trickle through her fingers Ningermaner felt a kinship with each grain of sand: a kinship stronger here than in any other place, forever calling her back to the bay of her birth. It was good to be back again in the Seafood Land to hear again the rhythmic slap of the waves on the beach and the calls of the seabirds.

Ningermaner was content to doze in the warm sand dunes after the long journey. Afterwards she would slip away to talk to her sacred tree. It too was getting old like her. It looked more weatherbeaten each season, but she felt closer to her real self beside it than by any other tree. Later she would call the children together and go through the ancient Sea songs and dances which belonged to Common Knowledge.

Twilight was the best time for sitting still. Now was a play time for the older children and a sleeping time for the babies.

The old woman settled herself down to watch over Moonah's new girl-child and Nunnelarie's twins, while the men went inland to hunt. The women went to the rocky headland, some to dive for crayfish and others to look for signs of seals and penguins.

Sun shone warm; presently the babies were asleep. The old woman's own eyes became heavy like those of the blue-tongued lizard. Through half-closed lids she watched the older children as one of Manganinnie's boys rolled a ball of kelp down a sandy bank and the other children tried to spear it with their small spears. The soft warm dunes rang with their laughter as they played their hunting game.

Ningermaner watched Dreenee with pride. It was good to see him playing with the other children. So often he wandered away on his own. Fondly the old woman's eyes followed his long lean limbs as he played the spearing game. How fast he had grown!

He was bigger than Lugga and other boys his own age and could handle his small spear with extreme speed and accuracy. Children older than himself were playing the game his way.

Listening to the message of Sea and the faraway laughter of the children, Ningermaner's eyelids grew heavier. Soon she too was fast asleep.

Sun hung low in Sky, pausing to make long shadows before he painted Sky with red ochre, and Dreenee paused to marvel at his own long shadow. Soon he would be as tall as the men! He was looking at the long running shadows of the other children when he noticed other shadows on the sand. Looking up he saw his magpies, circling overhead. Something must be very wrong, for they looked flustered and were chortling a very urgent Travel Song.

Dreenee looked across the sands to the other children, but they didn't appear to notice the magpies; there were many birds about. He looked towards the place where the women were diving. Sea was smooth as a seal's back and three women were laughing as they surfaced with crayfish in their hands. He glanced towards the smoke of the campfire, where Ningermaner was minding the babies and he could see that they were all asleep.

Before he was fully aware of his actions he slithered behind a sand dune and sped away, the urgent Travel Song of the magpies ringing in his ears as his legs carried him along the beach and through the thicket of tea-tree and she-oak.

Wind was strong, pushing him from behind as he scrambled up to the steep headland where the magpies had already landed. He could see them strutting and running about, the black and white patches of their feathers ruffled by the strong wind. They really seemed very agitated.

His heart pounding, Dreenee scaled the last ledge and joined his waiting magpies. His eyes scanned the empty sea and the magpies tried to make their wind-blown half circle around him. He looked back towards the camp and could see the smoke curling from his People's fire, and then moving closer to the face of the cliff he looked down into the next bay. On the distant rocks he could see a family of seals basking in the sun — and moving rapidly across the bay was a long-boat with two pale-faced men! They were moving quite fast into the wind.

Hardly had Dreenee taken in all that he had seen when the magpies reeled off into the sky and flew back to the reef where the women were diving. Dreenee's whole body trembled as it knew the danger and felt the fear. He had heard through Common Knowledge of the sealers who stole women. It had happened to other tribes, so the councillors now ordered that someone keep watch when the women were diving. He could see no look-about man or woman.

Leaping and sliding the young boy crashed through the small bushes and over the sand dunes.

"Wake Ningermaner! Wake Ningermaner!" he sobbed to his magpies; but it was hopeless. Wind took the words from his lips and blew them out to Sea.

Leaning into Wind Dreenee raced on, but already he could see the boat rounding the headland ahead of him and gliding quietly towards the place where the women were diving. His own mother had just come up to the surface; and while he ran the other two women dived again.

Moonah did not hear the boat until it was almost beside her, for Wind was blowing their sound away from her. She screamed and dived but there was no-one to hear her. Nunnelarie and Longameena had already returned to the silent underwater feeding place of the crayfish. She dived deep and swam underwater to a hiding place between some rocks. Here she made the call of the black cockatoo, which would alert the People.

She could hear strange loud voices and splashing and she could hear Nunnelarie's screams. Moonah dived again and swam closer, hiding behind more rocks. She could now see Nunnelarie being roughly hauled into the boat by one man while the other man was pulling on the end of a thick stick. The stick had a long curved hook on it and held Longameena by the arm.

Quickly Moonah hurled a stone at the man's head and he fell sideways into the boat. She hurled another stone at the second man, but it was too late. Already the boat was moving away. She could see Nunnelarie sink her teeth into the man's arm and heard him bellow, but he was too strong for her.

On the shore Moonah could see her People rushing about, but it was too late. All they could do was throw stones, brandish spears and yell as the boat carried Nunnelarie over the rim of their world.

Moonah looked about for signs of Longameena. The boat hook, she noticed, had floated to the beach, but she could not find Longameena! Sun was slipping away fast. Moonah was frantically swimming about and diving. Then she found blood-stained water and, diving deep, found her.

It was a silent suffering group who gathered around the still body of Longameena when Moonah brought her ashore. The arm was bleeding and twisted, there was a bump on her head and her eyes stared back from an empty face. No breath came from the blue lips.

Dreenee stood as if in a dream as the People tipped Longameena up and drained the water from her lungs. Someone was wrapping her in kangaroo skins and another was packing the wound with ashes and binding it with layers of bark.

All Dreenee wanted to do was to cling to his mother, but Moonah was too busy. Ningermaner was busy also, so he moved away to the other side of the campfire, bewildered by all that had happened so quickly. Here he had time to think and slowly he became aware of Nunnelarie's twins who were crying for their milk. A cold chill ran down his spine as he realised that their mother had been stolen. Who would feed them now? He took them in his arms, rocking out some of his own pain as he gazed across the fire to the place where Longameena lay, her bruised head cradled on his own mother's thighs.

His little sister was now crying, but Dreenee realised that she would now have to wait her turn and share her mother's milk with the twins.

Dreenee could hear the men talking earnestly together. They were planning to move camp at first light. Nunnelarie's husband was rocking to and fro, hitting his head against a rock to ease the pain of his loss.

No-one had thought of the evening meal or milk for the babies, so Dreenee carried the twins over to their father and then gave his little sister a piece of pig-face to suck. Next he began to roast a young wallaby, and seeing this, Lugga came to help. Cooking was always done by the women, but tonight it would be different.

There were now only three women in this group and perhaps one of them was going to die — or was she already dead? Dreenee did not know — and the three babies needed milk. Only his mother had milk.

As Dreenee singed the fur off the wallaby he talked about these things to Lugga. Then, gazing into the glowing coals, speaking softly, he called up the tiny Fire spirits, pleading for help.

Fire hissed and spat as the meat cooked, and the smell of food filled the air, taking away some of the pain.

Moon flooded the dunes as she climbed higher and higher and peeping down saw Longameena stir and open her eyes. Moon could see Nunnelarie's husband sitting alone, sharpening his spears, bewilderment and rage shining in his eyes; and she could see away over the sea to the island where Nunnelarie had been taken.

Moon looked to the place where the three babies were

moving restlessly but knew that Moonah had given them all the milk she could. She blessed Moonah from her place high in the Sky, continuing to move slowly across it with a sad heart. Every season there were fewer People gathering to watch and wait for her to grow fat and round.

23. Emu Eggs

Dawn cast a rosy hue over the dunes as the small band moved away from the sad place. Following the ancient pathway they travelled inland to the big lagoon; all except Nunnelarie's husband. He had left earlier to look for signs of the white men's boat.

Dreenee's heart was heavy as he followed the others. Moonah was now carrying two babies on her back and Ningermaner the third one. Ningermaner went on ahead, while two warriors carried Longameena on a thick piece of bark. Sometimes she moaned and this worried Dreenee. He watched his mother's face but there was no smile in her eyes. Ningermaner's face showed no expression; her mind was far away. Even Lugga and the other boys were quiet. Normally they would be throwing stones or laughing.

In single file the little band followed Mannerganner across the flat, wet marsh where bullfrogs croaked and native hens scattered raucously before them. Overhead swamp hawks hunted. Food was plentiful. Goannas and snakes sunned themselves, well hidden in the bullrushes and silver tussocks. The marsupial mice and rat-kangaroos nested in the yellow sedges, but no-one was interested in food.

Dreenee lagged a short distance behind the People, reading tracks and listening and seeing much food. He was hungry and lonely, but no-one seemed to care.

In a clump of tea-tree he saw movement and heard a deep rumble. He threw a stone into the clump and an emu blundered to its feet and strutted off with huge startled strides. At a safe distance it stopped, compelled by its curiosity to look again.

Dreenee made the deep rumbling noise of the emu and the big bird stared back in his direction, its head swinging from side to side as it tried to locate the sound. Emu would often move quite close if everyone stood still and mimicked the call. It was an amusing game — one all the children enjoyed. But no-one was interested today, not even Lugga.

Dreenee wished that he had a big spear and was strong enough to carry the emu. He looked at his shadow and knew it would be many moons yet before this would be possible. Perhaps there would be eggs where the bird had been squatting? He was very hungry.

Leaving the track he went over to the place and sure enough there were several big green eggs. With a sharp stick he knocked a small hole in one of the eggs and sucked furiously at the lovely warm food. Then he tried to carry the others. He could hold one in each hand, but there were still two more eggs. He tucked one in each armpit and hurried away with all four eggs.

Soon he joined the party, feeling much better. Moonah saw the eggs and smiled gently.

24. Goat's Milk

The sky was busy with birds around the lagoon and Sun was warm. The children frolicked about in the water looking for birds' eggs while Moonah fed the babies and Ningermaner nursed Longameena. Dreenee, seeing a small flock of magpies, left the water to listen. They were chortling the same Travel Song he had heard only yesterday. It wasn't such an urgent song this time, but he knew it was important.

The youngster raced away around the lagoon, following the birds. Quite soon his magpies circled around. Stealthily he peered through the undergrowth and saw a clearing made by white man and a rough wooden hut. He slithered behind a burnt log to look and listen and close by the magpies strutted about, feeding on insects. Sometimes they ran around, but they did not fly away and Dreenee, watching them, knew that he was meant to stay.

Smoke came from the rough chimney and on a line some clothes flapped in the gentle breeze. Studying the clothes and watching the door at the same time, Dreenee noticed trousers and shirts and also the long dress of calico which told him a woman lived in the hut. How he longed to take the blue dress back to camp for his mother! His fingers ached with wanting. He planned his approach and moved slowly forward, but the magpies ruffled their feathers and ran in front of him. Their fiery eyes looked almost angry. Dreenee was confused.

"So you want me to wait, do you?" he asked, and watched as the expression of anger faded from their eyes.

Dreenee did not have long to wait. From his hiding place he saw a white woman come out of the door and collect the clothes. He was sorry to see the bright dress taken inside, but there were other things to see. Tied to a tree by a long rope was one of their new animals and he remembered it was called 'Goat'. Alice had given him the name when they had been looking at her picture book.

"Goat", he said softly, pleased with himself for remembering the word. The animal was smaller than Cow, which he had seen before, but otherwise it was the same shape and it looked as though it gave milk like Cow.

Moments later the woman came outside again with a bucket in her hand and walked across to the new animal. Quietly she untied the rope and led it to a place with plenty of grass and then she started milking. She was quite close to Dreenee, and he could hear the swish of the milk into the bucket and he could smell the warm sweet smell.

He looked to his magpies, and could see the gentle light was still in their eyes. They ran about fussing and warbling as they fed on insects, but they did not fly away. He realised that the magpies were thinking about taking the milk back to the babies. His eyes glowed as he planned.

Sun walked with Dreenee, warm as feathers on his body as he followed the creek, leading the goat. Sometimes he had to pull and sometimes he had to push her, but at last he got her over the creek, and then it was only a short distance back to camp.

Soon he was there. Carefully he tied Goat to a tree, and called to the People. His face was glowing with excitement as he told them he had milk for the babies but Dreenee's smile was soon to fade as he saw amazement turn to anger on his mother's face. Soon everyone was shouting at him. He was placed on a low branch of a tree, then everyone pointed at him and jeered.

Sun did not care to look upon the pain in Dreenee's eyes, so he slipped behind a cloud while the People jeered. Moonah untied the rope and led Goat away.

Mannerganner watched Goat being hurried away, but he said nothing. Dreenee still belonged to the women and it was the women's job to punish him. He collected his warriors together and studied the cloven footprints made by the new animal and stored them in his mind. Then he quietly ordered everyone to move camp to the other side of the lagoon.

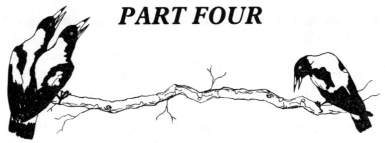

PART FOUR

25. Alice is Lost

Spring was in the air as the People moved inland. Following the flight of *warrah* the duck they walked away from the Seafood Land leaving behind all hope of ever seeing Nunnelarie again, but glad that Longameena had recovered from her dreadful ordeal. As the days lengthened the ancient rhythm of the Motherland called them up into the Land of Many Lakes for the Eggfood Season and as summer faded into autumn and the swallows flew out to sea, the unchanging cycle of migration led them down to the lowland rivers and gullies.

When snow covered the great proud boulders and blizzards of sleet squalled over the lakes and tarns in the highlands, and food was scarce, the people were hunting their ways along the rivers and gullies of the lowlands.

Night was dark before dawn. The People slept close together, sharing the warmth of each other and their kangaroo skins. Outside each simple bark shelter a small fire glowed and crumbled in the cold night air. Night animals prowled and snarled, or silently padded about in search of food; and in the dark places Evil Spirits lurked.

The rhythm of Night flowed over Droemerdeene's Land while the People slept.

Suddenly Dreenee stirred and woke. He could hear magpies warbling! Even as he listened the sounds came nearer.

It was very dark, and he was afraid. None of the People travelled at night for fear of the Evil Spirits. Surely the magpies didn't want him to follow them in the dark? Fear clutched at him with clammy hands, making his whole body shudder.

He closed his eyes very tightly and curled up small. He then tried to close his ears, but somehow they wouldn't close and his eyes wouldn't stay shut. Somewhere out in the darkness some creature needed help and the big birds had come to him. He could see the shadowy outlines of five magpies flutter down and settle silently in the silver tussocks beyond the glowing campfire. He had to follow them.

With trembling fingers, Dreenee selected a stout piece of honeysuckle wood and kindled it from Fire. In no time he was feeling his way through the dark, his eyes wide with fear and just in front of him the magpies hovered and flew, chortling urgently.

Soon Dreenee's eyes became accustomed to the dark and he could see the outlines of the trees. Merry little fire spirits twinkled and twirled in the glow of his firestick, taking away the terror of Night. He began to carol to show how brave he was and the birds joined in, warbling sweetly, crowding out the noises of the night animals and hunting away the Evil Spirits who dwelt in the dark places.

At last, when he was almost out of breath, they came to a wild cherry tree gully, and here the magpies settled down on the ground and formed a circle around a pile of something which moved and moaned. The youngster stood motionless, looking and listening. His legs shook now, not from the fast running, but from fear of the unknown thing on the ground.

Trembling, he blew on his firestick. Then, holding it high, he recognised the little white girl.

"Alice!" he said aloud, scarcely able to believe his eyes. He felt her clothes and they were only damp from rain. Her hands, however, were very cold and she did not hear her name.

Quickly Dreenee collected dry bark and dead wood from under a gum tree, and while he worked the magpies warbled softly around Alice.

Dreenee could now see much better. Long flickering

flames flared as they licked the bark and twigs. Soon they were eating into the thick pieces of wood and he could see that Alice's face was very pale. Her clothes were muddy and she even had mud on her face. Her eyes were closed, but sometimes her head moved as she moaned.

Dreenee was at a loss to know what to do. He had no skin to keep Alice warm, only Fire, so first he busied himself making another one behind her, and then he collected some damp moss from the ice-cold creek and washed the mud away from her eyes and mouth.

As Dreenee worked, he wondered how Alice could have fallen over. She did not answer when he spoke her name. She only moaned; the moaning worried him. Then he noticed that one of her legs was twisted. Gently he fumbled with the cord until he had got rid of the stupid tight boot. Now he could see what was really wrong. Her foot was swollen. He must get more water and moss and bathe it, and afterwards some thick bark to bind round it so as to stop it falling sideways. Being busy was much better than waiting.

As Dreenee gathered moss, water and bark he found the round circular mark which told him of a small Horse beyond the ferns where Alice lay. There was a caved-in burrow of a wombat where Horse had apparently stumbled, throwing Alice forward onto the ground. When she had fallen she hurt her ankle. The prints showed that she had tried to hobble along. Horse must have gone back to the settlement.

The day dawned clear and crisp after the cold wet night. Soon Dreenee could hear the long drawn out cooee sounds and the ringing of a bell, far away. Cupping his hands to his mouth he made a mimicking sound in the direction of the cooee, but even as he made the new call he doubted if they would hear him. They didn't hear as well as his People and it was unlikely that they could find the tracks of Horse after last night's shower. Alice was nearly as big as he was and he knew that he could not carry her; yet he did not like to leave her.

Even as the young boy pondered and planned, the magpies moved closer and settled in the nearby trees. They stared at him silently, their eyes growing brighter, but all Dreenee could do was to stare back at them, wishing them even closer. Dreenee's mind became empty as the kind old leader fluttered down very near him and slowly he could feel the magpie-magic working. He realised that he had managed to 'think' the old magpie closer, so why couldn't he 'think' Ningermaner closer, simply by wishing very hard?

Dreenee closed his mind to everything but Ningermaner.

26. Dreenee to the Rescue

Ningermaner woke with a start. Her shoulder was twitching intently, yet it was still rather dark. Dawn was only just beginning to creep over the Land. Listening with her inside ear, she heard Dreenee's spirit calling her again and again. She looked at his sleeping place and, finding it empty, took a firestick and a kangaroo skin and slipped away from the camp, following his tracks.

While she was looking for the tracks, peering close to the ground in the gentle half-light of the early dawn, she heard a strange cooee call which did not belong to the birds or to the creatures of Night. Then she heard a ringing sound far off and remembered the bell she had heard once on a cow at a trapper's hut. The two noises must belong to the white people at the settlement; and somewhere Dreenee was needing help.

As the old woman felt her way through the grey shadows, she summoned her help-spirits:

"Take me to Dreenee. I must get to him quickly, but his tracks are hard to see in this light."

Early morning mist hung in the gullies and in the pale grey outlines of the mighty gums. Tree spirits began to twinkle, lighting up the way for Ningermaner, until at last she could see the glow of a fire in the distance. She stopped at once and made the bird-call of the black cockatoo and in a matter of moments Dreenee replied.

Ningermaner's head was clear and wide awake as she approached the light of Fire. Gliding stealthily from one tree to another and keeping to the high ground, the old woman moved closer, looking and listening for signs of trouble. Tightly fisted in each hand she held a round throwing stone. Perhaps her grandson had been captured again by the newcomers? This place was quite near a settlement.

Softly she called to Dreenee and in a few moments he was racing towards her. Relief flooded over Ningermaner when she saw him. She squatted down under a gum, listening carefully as he told her what had happened.

She needed time to think and plan how best she and Dreenee could get Alice home to her family without being captured themselves. Even now she could hear the not-so-distant bell ringing and the calls coming once more. Calmly she told Dreenee to climb a tree and keep watch. This done, she scrambled down the rocky slope and bent over the little white girl.

How pale her skin was! Ningermaner's eyes were wide with wonder as they scanned the limp body. She had never seen such a pale human being!

She observed what her grandson had already done for the unconscious child and she felt very proud of him.

"Well done, Dreenee", she called to him in his place up the tree, and then she removed Alice's wet clothes and wrapped the kangaroo skin carefully around the little girl and moved her closer to the embers. Gently Ningermaner bathed Alice's face and then rubbed her cold little hands, calling to her. At last, Alice's eyes opened.

The soft dawn swelled into brilliant colours as Ningermaner carried Alice down towards the Wide River. Going ahead, Dreenee followed the now-faint hoof prints of Horse. Overhead the trees were noisy with birds after the wet refreshing rain, but he did not heed them, for his mind was absorbed with looking and listening. He could hear the ringing and also the cooee call which was much closer now.

He was really pleased that he had been able to call up Ningermaner! Perhaps he could put a Hiding Spell around them as they travelled?

Pointing his firestick at a thick blanket of fog which curled low over the creek, he summoned it to him. As he watched it drifted towards them and wrapped itself around the little party in a soft grey circle.

The small party climbed out of the next gully still safely hidden in mist and, looking down, saw the white man's house beside the Wide River. Ningermaner concealed herself carefully in a dense thicket of wattles and gently put Alice down on the ground. Dreenee wanted to race away down to the fence and call out, but Ningermaner was very firm.

"No, we will look and listen. Alice is all right", she told him.

The young boy settled restlessly beside her. Ningermaner seldom said "No", and he knew that she really meant it this time.

A cow could be heard and the cackling of hens, but there was no sign of people. Dreenee climbed a small tree and from there he could see over the fence and into the settlement. He could see a little horse, but there was no sign of the big one he had ridden with Thomas, and the dog was nowhere to be seen. Smoke came from the chimney but it seemed no people were about. The cooee sound came again, echoing across the hills.

Dreenee swung down from the tree and told Ningermaner what he had seen and after a while she decided that it would be safe for him to cooee. Three times Dreenee cooeed, loud enough to be heard at the house. Intently they looked and listened for signs of people, but there was no response. The only sounds were an occasional moan from Alice and the cackling of hens and the bellowing of a cow behind the paling fence. Now was the time to get Alice inside the fence.

Dreenee was given strict instructions to stay in the tree and keep watch and then Ningermaner picked up the little girl and moved towards the white man's house. She reached the fence and struggled to open the gate.

From his look-out Dreenee could see in all directions, and as he held his breath watching Ningermaner he suddenly saw Alice's mother racing through the timber towards the house. She was calling frantically, "Alice!, Alice!" Evidently she had seen Ningermaner from another hill and she was racing home!

Dreenee's heart pounded as he saw Ningermaner dart inside the gate and put Alice down gently on the grass. Already Alice's mother had reached the creek. Her lovely red hair streamed behind her as she waded through the shallow water, and her long wet skirt clung to her legs and slowed her progress.

Desperately Dreenee gave the bird-call alarm. He could see Ningermaner pause, looking at some ducks hanging upside-down in a tree, when she should be running out of the gateway, and he realised that she had not heard Alice's mother.

Suddenly everything was happening too fast. Hens were running everywhere, cackling; the two cows were rushing through the open gateway, tight bags of milk swinging from side to side; and coming up behind Dreenee was Pungertenner! Pungertenner, whom he hadn't seen since his capture at the settlement! Evidently she had seen Ningermaner and Alice from another ridge but had not yet seen Dreenee in the tree.

He called to her urgently and she stopped, utterly amazed, and came to him just as Ningermaner darted out through the gateway and came running up the hill towards them. A few moments later Alice's mother reached the open gateway.

Ningermaner flopped down under the wattles. She had had a nasty fright near the gate and her old legs trembled from so much running, but she smiled as she waited for her breathing to slow down. She was pleased with Dreenee for making the warning call (her curiosity about the four ducks could well have got her into trouble).

"Dreenee", she called, and to her amazement he appeared with a strange black girl beside him! The women gazed at one another, then all together they turned to look down beyond the fence where Alice's mother was now crouching over her little girl, examining the splint on her foot.

Ningermaner spoke quietly to Pungertenner, hoping to learn who she was. Dreenee's eyes moved intently from one face to the other, understanding the difference in their tribal dialects and marvelling at the communication Ningermaner achieved through her open gestures and pleading tones.

"Soon we will travel to the Seafood Land again; you can come with us! Your own People will be there for the festival and many young men will come to woo you with flowers and shell necklaces."

Pungertenner was smiling pensively. Then she turned to Dreenee and patting him fondly on the head she asked, "Bread and butter and jam?"

The boy looked longingly at Pungertenner, and in her own eyes he also saw confusion and a mixture of wanting to come and wanting to stay.

She smiled and said "Good boy", and then she said "Dreenee, horse?"

Dreenee beamed at the very thought of having another ride on Horse. He laughed and jumped about yelling "Horse, Horse!", but when he looked for Ningermaner to share his excitement she had walked away, further up the hill. Reluctantly he followed her, gazing back over his shoulder at Pungertenner who smiled and waved her hand high in the manner of the white people.

Sun was walking across the top of the sky when the old woman and her grandson arrived back in camp. As Ningermaner expected, there was no-one about, the men having gone off to hunt wallabies and the women and children to collect small animals and dig for tubers, or to sleep under the trees while the children played in the river. After all the excitement the old woman was quite glad to lie down by her fire but Dreenee was far too restless to sleep and much too hungry after his long night, so he went off to collect his hidden Pot and hunt for eggs.

Later, he had Pot on the fire and was waiting for the water to boil. Singing happily he put the eggs in when it was bubbling.

Still Ningermaner slept, so when the eggs were cooked he ate them all himself. Afterwards he returned Pot to the special hiding place in the river. When the People returned to camp, Ningermaner and Dreenee were both fast asleep.

The men had speared two wallabies and soon the smell of roasting meat filled the camp.

The meal was nearly over when Dreenee and the old woman woke. After eating, Ningermaner gathered all the women round her and told them what she and Dreenee had been doing. When she had finished the talk became general, the old men questioning her carefully about the Settlement, and the young men wanting to know more and more about Pungertenner.

Dreenee watched the crafty eyes of Ningermaner and he felt happier as he looked inside them. He was almost sure that she would not tell the People about the stolen pot today, but just to be sure he put a little spell about her. It was only a very small spell, like a cobweb, but it worked.

27. In Honour of Dreenee

Pungertenner was restless as she moved about the house. She thought approvingly of Dreenee, and the memory of his beautiful wide smile kindled a warm glow in her eyes as she pulled the big iron bell calling her master and Thomas home. Memories of her own childhood, tucked away in the dim recesses of her mind, flooded back again and moved with her as she stoked the fire and heated the kettles. Alice was still very cold and her mistress was calling for a bathtub and for bricks to be placed on the hob for warming the bed. Porridge must be made as quickly as possible too, and a teaspoon of brandy mixed with warm milk and sugar for Alice to drink.

Her body weary from the long disturbed night, Pungertenner moved listlessly from one task to the next, but her mind was far away as she cooked the porridge and watched as Alice moaned and came awake and then drifted back to sleep. Her own thoughts were back in that clump of wattles with Dreenee and Ningermaner.

Only when Alice was lifted into the bathtub of warm water did she awake fully, crying, "Mama! Mama! Where is Dreenee? I want Dreenee!"

Tears welled in the eyes of her mother as Alice spoke, and she held her tightly in her arms while great sobs of relief flooded over her. Her face was white after the sleepless night of searching, her beautiful long red hair was dishevelled and her clothes crumpled and torn. Compassion gleamed in Pungertenner's deepset eyes and a need of her own stirred and washed over her.

Certainly she loved little Alice and Tom. Had she not watched them learn to walk and run, and later to climb and ride? Yet suddenly she realised that they could never take the place of her own People. She thought of Dreenee's beautiful smile and she felt really proud. But for him, surely Alice would have perished in last night's cold! She could feel a song welling up inside her, a song about Dreenee, but now she must make tea for her mistress and wrap the hot bricks in thick flannel to warm the bed. The danger was over. Her master and Thomas would hear the bell and soon be home. They would be tired and hungry.

So weary and deep in thought was Pungertenner as she pondered over her dawning need for children of her own that she didn't hear her mistress call her from the bedroom. She stoked the kitchen fire and hung a big pot of soup over the flames; but her mind was far away.

"Quickly, Maria! Give me the hot bricks. Where are the

flannels? Alice is still very cold. Ring the bell again. Get more bricks in the fire!"

"Yes, Ma'am. Maybe you should get into bed with Alice. You could keep her warm, while I heat more bricks."

Suddenly the kitchen door swung open and the Master rushed inside, with Thomas close behind.

"Lizzie! Where is Alice? Have you found her?"

"She's in our bed, but we must keep our voices down, because . . ." A weary smile trembled on her lips and she leaned into his arms, almost too tired for words.

"Lizzie, my dear! Where did you find her?"

"An old woman carried her home."

"An old woman? Who? Not a native?"

"Yes, my love. It's true, Edward. A wonderful old woman", Lizzie said, and began to sob.

Gently Edward picked her up and carried her into the bedroom. Thomas was already there, his face close to Alice's. They sat together on the bed, whispering her name and thanking God and the old woman for finding their little girl.

"We are lucky she didn't take Alice back to her tribe, aren't we, Papa? After all, we did take Dreenee away from his family. I can imagine how surprised they would be — just as curious as we were about Dreenee. They would probably laugh at her clothes . . ."

"Hush, hush, Thomas", his father implored. He could feel his wife's body tremble. Moments later she was sobbing out all her pent-up emotion.

Thomas hugged his mother. He had never seen her cry like this. He felt confused and tired and very hungry.

"Your mother's shoes are wet, Thomas. Can you take them off? Then we'll all have a brandy. It will warm us up. Yes, you too!"

Edward smiled fondly as he watched the anguish on Thomas's face change to joy. "You have earned your first brandy. After last night's ordeal you are my right hand man now," he whispered.

Together they sat around the kitchen fire, sipping brandy while Maria busied herself carving meat.

"Tell us about the old Aborigine, Lizzie. Did you see her?"

"Oh, yes! But when she saw me she ran away and disappeared among the wattles."

"And what made you come home?"

"I heard a cooee when I was in the next gully. It seemed to come from this direction, so I hurried home. I actually saw her carry Alice down towards the gate. Oh, Edward!" Lizzie smiled for the first time in two days.

"What was she like?" Thomas asked. "I'd love to meet her and know her name. We could give her a present, couldn't we, Papa? And thank her."

"Perhaps," Edward thought to himself, "Maria may have seen her."

"Maria," he said kindly, "did you see the old woman?"

"Yes, master, I also heard the call and came rushing home. I even talked to her a little. Her name is Ningermaner . . ." Pungertenner paused. "Dreenee was with her, so I said 'thank you,' and he understood. I even tried to persuade him to live with us, but Ningermaner hurried him away."

"Dreenee?", Thomas said, sipping his small glass of brandy and hot milk. Already he felt warm inside. "I wonder if Dreenee would come and live with us?"

Pungertenner watched while they had their brandy. She too was cold and weary; yet no-one offered her brandy. Accepting the fact, she moved about the kitchen preparing food for her master's family but nevertheless an empty feeling welled up inside her. "If I could say 'thank you' to Ningermaner, surely my master could have said 'thank you, Maria'? Even that dreadful name Maria would be better than being almost ignored. A sip of brandy would . . ." Her thoughts were interrupted.

"Maria, how do you say the old woman's name again?" her master had spoken.

"Ningermaner," she said, very slowly.

Soon Edward and Lizzie and young Thomas were raising their glasses. "To Ningermaner!" Edward said, "God bless her soul!"

"To Ningermaner!" echoed Lizzie and Thomas but for Thomas the name sounded fuzzy, and Edward, watching him, decided it was time for soup and bed.

"What about Dreenee?" Thomas asked. "I bet he helped!" So a toast was drunk to Dreenee, and feeling light-headed but very pleased with himself, Thomas devoured his soup. Then he yawned and moments later he was fast asleep at the table.

28. Pungertenner Escapes

Soon the house was silent as everyone slept — all except Pungertenner. The clock on the mantelpiece ticked away the daylight hours. It was now three o'clock and the cow hadn't been milked since yesterday. The chooks hadn't been fed, and the eggs must be collected, and there were still dishes to be washed and wood to be brought in for the fire.

Her body was weary and her mind drifted back along the gully where she had last seen Ningermaner and Dreenee. Pungertenner felt lonely. All night she had searched for Alice, but no-one had told her to go and sleep. She did not truly belong with these people; she did not really know where she belonged!

Pungertenner let her thoughts drift back over her young life. She had been stolen by sealers as a very young woman, but their boat had been wrecked on a reef almost immediately. She had been rescued by other white people and taken to Hobart Town. Here she had been made to work for one person after another until finally she had run away, and a kind man on a small grey pony had found her, alone and hungry, hiding in a hollow tree. He had told her that God had sent him to look for her and that God was with them.

This had been very confusing for her, because there was no sign of 'God'; there was only the kind man and a little grey pony which left fascinating footprints in the mud. The man told her his name was Robert Knopwood and that he would find a nice home for her. He told her a lot about God and asked her questions about her own People and what they knew of God, but Pungertenner could only tell him about the Stars and Sun and Moon, and point to where the Ancestral Beings lived in the sky. Robert Knopwood said that God also lived in the sky but, hard as she tried, she could not see him.

Understanding about God had been very difficult, but she was glad that he had sent this kind man who took her home to his cottage and gave her food and clothes. The next day they had set off on the same little pony, whose name was Timor, and followed the track along the banks of the Wide River until they came to a house where a white man and woman lived with children named Thomas and Alice.

After that day Pungertenner had known only kindness, and over the years she had become one of the family — or had she? Did she really belong here? Seeing Dreenee again had made her so happy, and meeting Ningermaner for the first time and listening to her had only made the longing for her own People surface and grow strong.

Weariness and confusion mingled, walking with her as she went outside to feed the animals and collect the eggs.

High in the yellow gums a colony of black and white magpies stared at Pungertenner as she filled a bucket with water and then all together they carolled loudly. Much to the young woman's amazement she felt compelled to stop and listen to them. As if in a trance she put the bucket down and walked over to their tree, her eyes never leaving them. She completely forgot about feeding the animals.

Settling herself down in the shade of the yellow gum Pungertenner listened to the various warbling notes of each bird blend together to become an urgent chortle; and it was almost as though she could understand them! It was a nice warm feeling, for she knew they needed her in some way.

She could feel their thoughts flowing into her mind simply by being near, but she was very tired and could not quite understand them. She could only sense their urgent need.

Then the old leader fluttered down beside her, his eyes shining brighter than firelight, and all the other birds followed him. Soon they were making a black and white circle around her on the ground. Silently each bird stared at her. They were much closer now, and their message flowed easily into her mind. She must sleep and then tomorrow she must follow them to Ningermaner, as her own People needed her; and, she realised at last, she needed them.

Through heavy lids Pungertenner watched as the magpies flapped their wings and fluttered away. She wanted time to think. She rather liked wearing clothes like her mistress and sleeping in a warm bed on cold wet nights; yet it would be wonderful to sing and dance with her own People and to have her own man.

She recalled Ningermaner gliding away through the wattles towards the morning sun and she heard again her plea: "This is no place for a beautiful young woman like you. We Big River People need you. We must learn more about the ways of the white people, and you have much to teach us . . . If you will not come with me now, the magpies will be waiting for you in the yellow gums, and you can travel safely with them to our camp."

The meaning of Ningermaner's words washed over the young woman, soothing as the liquid music of a gurgling creek, and her eyelids grew heavy. The cows had yet to be milked and the fire tended, yet sleep was drifting over her softly, and the gentle words of the old woman were mingling with the song of the magpies. Soon the two sounds melted together and Pungertenner slept while Sun walked across the top of Sky.

That night, alone in her bed, Pungertenner tossed fitfully, and when she did sleep her dreams were full of the songs of her People.

The first pale shafts of early morning light were edging through her window when she woke. Nearby a rooster crowed and far away she could hear the morning song of the magpies. She looked about her little room and overhead to the rafters which blocked out a view of the ancient stars, and suddenly she longed for the unfenced places and the flickering firelight of her dreams.

Quickly she slid out of bed and dressed herself. Then on noiseless feet she slipped away out of the silent, sleeping house and through the gate just as Sun touched the pale shadowy arms of the big yellow gums, painting them gold.

There was a flutter of black and white wings as the magpies circled overhead, warbling sweetly before flying down along the gully.

"Come away, come away, Pungertenner," they seemed to sing as they settled down beside the creek. With their singing, joy filled her heart.

On long black legs with her skirt held high, Pungertenner bounded down towards the creek and swiftly made her way towards the camp of the People.

29. Careful Planning

Ningermaner's shoulder was twitching when she woke, and she knew that her help-spirits were pointing the way for Pungertenner.

Excitement glowed in her eyes as she scrambled to her feet. Today would be a very special day for her family and so it must be carefully planned. She was the first to wake; this was good because she needed time to herself.

All her cunning and authority would be needed if Pungertenner was to be accepted without fuss and fighting. Mannerganner, she knew, would be angry that he had not been told; but it was better this way. Several secret meetings had been held by the men since Ningermaner had spoken with Pungertenner at the white man's house and she knew that the men had become curious; probably they were already planning to steal her.

Ningermaner did not approve of fighting. The very thought of the men attacking the house and possibly burning it down worried her. None of the women liked fighting, but of course they were never consulted. Planning in these things belonged to the men. There had been so much trouble already because the white men had killed and captured many of the People and invaded the hunting grounds. In retaliation her People had speared their sheep. The only way, Ningermaner thought again, was to learn as much as possible about the ways of the white people. Had not her husband come to her in the embers of her fire and told her so? It had clearly been her duty to encourage her to return to her people.

Pensively the old woman pushed the scattered embers of her fire together and then collected more wood. The fire must be large and bright as a fitting welcome to their visitor. Sun was peeping down into the gully and mist still hung in the low places. It was a beautiful pale morning, fresh-washed with rain and sparkling with dew.

Birds sang in the trees where the blossoms had now faded and the bright swollen berries shone with their message of approaching winter. Studying them, Ningermaner knew that soon it would be time to move down towards the sea again, while the highlands slept under soft white folds of snow. Tomorrow, or even today, Mannerganner might call them to move away, fearing that the white men would attack.

The old woman drank at the river and then she settled down by her fire to mix ashes from the hearth with wombat fat. Pungertenner would feel the cold after living inside a house for so long and wearing clothes. Every few days the People coated their bodies with fat. It was a wonderful way of keeping the cold out when the days got short and the sun grew weaker.

She sang softly to herself as she worked, mixing enough fat for Pungertenner as well as for herself. She then rubbed fat into her own body until her skin shone like the rain-washed trunk of the black wattle. And as she smeared the grease over the scars that she and all her People wore on their bodies as special marks of recognition, she wondered what markings Pungertenner wore. Perhaps, if she had been stolen a long time ago, she may not have any? She might even be too ashamed to discard her white man's clothes because to have no markings would mean she could not really belong to any tribe.

Concern showed in her deep set eyes as Ningermaner pondered. Perhaps she would give her a string of warrener shells and one of her baskets? She sorted through her treasures and found a lovely long string of shells and some red ochre. Next she made sure she had a sharp flint for shaving Pungertenner's untidy long hair.

Her shoulder was twitching more strongly now, so she knew for certain that Pungertenner was getting closer. It was time to waken Dreenee.

Dreenee uncurled himself when Ningermaner nudged him. He rubbed his eyes and scratched his head. Soon he was wide awake, and as he listened he could faintly hear his magpies. He looked about at the sleeping family and noticed that the fire was crackling merrily and that Ningermaner had smeared her body with grease. Now she was talking, not in the gentle sing-song voice he knew so well, but urgently with a bright gleam of excitement shining in her eyes.

"Go and look, Dreenee. Your magpies have a wonderful surprise for you. Today is a very special day."

Dreenee did not wait. He sped away in the direction of the settlement, leaping and bounding over fallen logs which stood in his way and crashing through the bracken ferns as if they were no more than cobwebs. There were magpies everywhere — not just one colony but several, so something very important must be happening! They seemed pleased to see him for they circled round him, warbling sweetly as they flew. When he was almost out of breath, they settled down on the top of a grassy bank and here they fussed about, snapping at grasshoppers.

Instinctively Dreenee waited too. He flattened himself in

116

the cool long grass and looked down the valley. In the distance he could see someone dressed in bright clothes, daintily stepping over a creek, her long skirt held high, and just in front of her, a colony of magpies circled! It was Pungertenner!

Dreenee blinked and looked again. He wanted to call out or rush down to her as fast as he could run, but he chewed on a juicy blade of grass and waited. If only he had brought a firestick! He could have given it to her as a gesture of welcome. He was scratching his head, wondering what he could give Pungertenner, when he saw a rosella watching him from her nest in a black stump.

"Feathers! Bright feathers! That is what I will give her!" he said. Keeping an eye on the figure approaching, Dreenee darted about looking for feathers.

When Pungertenner climbed out of the gully he was standing waiting for her, proud and straight, with a broad smile on his face; and in his outstretched hand a few brightly-coloured feathers. He swept one leg behind him and bowed low, and then carefully arranged the feathers in the young woman's hair.

Pungertenner's eyes almost overflowed with tears of joy as Dreenee took her hand and led her along the track to the camp. The feathers seemed to make her clothes look foolish, but for a long time now she had worn clothes and she was too shy to take them off. Alice was never allowed to run about without clothes, and her friend Robert Knopwood, who had often come to visit them, sometimes brought her a new dress. He also talked about the importance of wearing clothes and learning as much as possible about God. Yet Ningermaner did not wear clothes and she was very wise.

"Ningermaner?" she said with wide brown eyes looking straight at him, and Dreenee knew exactly what she was thinking, simply walking hand in hand with her. Silently he nodded, pointing in front of them, for he was lost for words under the spell of her beauty. Ningermaner, he thought to himself, would know what to do about the awful clothes. He would hate to see Pungertenner put in a tree and jeered at.

"Shoes?" he said, and Pungertenner smiled, for she too had been seeing inside his mind and knew his thoughts. Soon she was laughing as she squatted down, pulling off one shoe and then the other and handing them to Dreenee who stuffed them away in a stump.

Presently Pungertenner was also giving him long black stockings and pantaloons to hide; but somehow she couldn't bring herself to take off her red skirt and blouse. For too long she had been taught she must cover her body so, laughing to hide her confusion, she ran on ahead, her whole body trembling with the enormity of what she was doing. She was running away from the only life she had known for years, towards a very different life with her own People.

With no shoes to crowd her feet, her toes felt free and the feel of the soft damp earth made her want to leap for joy. Only when they came in sight of the camp did Dreenee and Pungertenner stop their joyous run. Suddenly the young woman trembled, seeing so many of her People. There were at least ten bark shelters and several campfires!

Pungertenner felt foolish wearing clothes, yet she could not take them off, so she dropped her eyes and squatted awkwardly, fingering her slim black toes while Dreenee walked over to Mannerganner and proudly said, "Pungertenner".

Suddenly the camp was like a babbling brook; women gabbled and yelled and little children appeared from everywhere. They raced over to stare at this strange young person with long hair and peculiar coverings.

Only the men were silent. With downcast eyes they gripped their spears tightly and moved closer to their Leader. Above all things they must not stare or show surprise. Their women, who were behaving so badly, would each be beaten later in private by their husbands.

It was a tense moment as Ningermaner walked forward and, sitting down next to Pungertenner, placed the shell necklace fondly around her neck and a bark tray of grease and ashes at her feet. Fiercely she glared at the women until they were silent and then she looked straight at Mannerganner. For one long moment there was complete silence. Then, pulling himself up to his full height, he spoke loudly and clearly.

"Who is this woman you call Pungertenner?"

Pungertenner could feel the nearness of Ningermaner, as with trembling fingers she fondled the little blue-green warrener shells, glad of her long hair which fell forward, hiding her face. A long time ago she had worn a necklace like this one. Slowly she fondled each precious shell, until it was almost as if her childhood family were quite close, and then she peeped out from behind her long black lashes. She listened to Ningermaner talking with great authority in the dialect which she did not fully understand. All eyes were on the old woman's face.

"Pungertenner has run away from white man's settlement and must travel with us to the Seafood Land and her tribal family."

After Ningermaner had spoken, Mannerganner moved forward and extended one leg behind him, bowing a formal greeting to Pungertenner. He knew he wanted to think very carefully about this new change, but in the meantime he must keep Ningermaner happy and answer as was expected of him. He was under her spell.

"It is good and proper that we should take this young woman into our band. She will have much to learn from us, and much to teach us. Now we move camp and Pungertenner will walk with Ningermaner, behind the rest. There is no time to waste, for the white man may already be following the footprints of Pungertenner."

30. Beyond the Mist

The clock in the kitchen struck seven, but no breakfast gong sounded in the silent house. The kitchen was a cold and empty place. No fire in the grate; no kettle boiling; no porridge simmering on the hob. Pungertenner was already running barefooted behind Dreenee along the native walk which would bring them to the camp of the Big River People.

When Thomas woke, his first thought was for his secret eel-trap. He simply must get down to the creek and back before his parents missed him. He only needed six more eels to fill the barrel. Then he would be the proud owner of a side-saddle, a present for his mother's birthday in two weeks. It was a race against time. Already he had lost two days while they were searching for Alice.

Pulling his clothes on, Thomas climbed out of the window and raced down to the creek. So intent was he on his eel-trap that he didn't notice the footprints of Pungertenner in the heavy frost, and when he came to the creek he didn't see the distant smoke. His hands were shaking as he pulled in the rope which was attached to the cask. The wooden cask was quite heavy! Carrying it over to his hiding place among the reeds, he tipped it upside-down, and much to his excitement four big eels wriggled about on the grass. Quickly he killed and skinned them. He knew that he was already late for breakfast, but he still needed time to get them into his secret barrel and salt them down and then, of course, bait and set his eel-trap again.

Thomas was about to wash and dry his skinned eels when the big bell rang three times. Three times meant a real emergency! What was wrong? Was Alice sick? Quickly he put his eels back in the cask, hoping the birds would leave them alone while he was away.

His mother looked stressed when Thomas rushed inside. "Where have you been, Thomas?"

He was about to say he had been searching for swans' nests when his father came in, looking very worried. Thomas knew he couldn't fib. Not now; not now that he was twelve. Quickly he said, "I was looking for eels."

"Yes, Thomas, we know you have been down to the creek. I followed your tracks. But what has kept you so long? Didn't you see Maria's footprints in the frost?"

"Maria's tracks?" Thomas queried, his eyes wide with

120

surprise. "No, Papa, I was running so I wouldn't be late for breakfast. Where is she?" "We think she has returned to her own people. Maybe she is just visiting them. We don't know. But we have been very worried about you. We thought you may have been stolen, or foolish enough to follow Maria. Just remember, Thomas, you need eyes in the back of your head in this country. It's not like England!", his father almost yelled.

"Come, come, Edward, don't upset yourself. Thomas is safe and that's what really matters. The last two days have been a dreadful strain on everyone."

"You are right, my love. Now we must decide what to do about Maria. Should I follow her tracks, or simply let her go?"

"But she can't go, Papa!" Thomas exclaimed. "We need her."

"Yes, son, I know we need her, but maybe she needs her people more than we need her. She is a young woman. She will be wanting her own husband and children. We cannot make her return, but what worries your mother and me is whether or not the Aborigines will accept her back into their tribe. Can she survive in the bush after having lived so long with us?" Edward stoked the fire and stirred the porridge, while Lizzie busied herself making toast and getting the eggs into a pot.

"Don't just stand there, Thomas!" she cried. "There's no time to waste. Set the table and then bring Alice in for breakfast!"

Thomas was glad to be busy. It was good to feel his little sister in his arms. The desperation of the search had given him strength to stay awake all night and tramp untold weary miles in the dark.

An awful feeling of guilt had walked with him! They had been double-dinking and he had got off Bess to release his homing pigeons. He should never have left Alice alone, because when the birds flew out of the box Bess had reared and cantered away . . .

Carefully he placed Alice in a chair while his mother

fussed around supporting the swollen ankle and feeling her toes. She had bandaged the leg last night without removing the old woman's splint. When Thomas saw it he was amazed and so was his father. They picked up the half cylinder of thick bark and studied the moss which lined it.

"How incredibly simple and effective!" Edward remarked.

"Yes, Edward, it looked so comfortable I didn't like to remove it last night."

"I bet even Dreenee could teach me lots of things about the bush," Thomas said.

"Yes, lad, it has been their home for thousands of years."

Edward paused, and then he smiled: "Even Dreenee would have seen Maria's tracks — and yours, leading from your window. They even met at the creek and were quite green in the frost."

Around the breakfast table they discussed what to do about Maria. Alice was most distressed when she realised that her special friend had gone. "Papa, please bring her home! She will be cold without a bed. She may even die. It was so cold and terrifying when it got dark after I had fallen off Bess."

Alice began to sob and Edward and Lizzie went over to her chair. "I will go and look for her, pet. You must try and sleep because you have had a dreadful shock. Now eat up your porridge like a brave girl and we'll talk about it when I get home." He stroked her hair and hurriedly finished his meal.

"Thomas, would you put those hot bricks in our bed, please?" Lizzie asked.

As soon as Thomas was out of hearing Lizzie told Edward that she guessed Thomas's thoughts: he wanted to go with his father. And he was still feeling very guilty about leaving Alice alone on the pony. "He has grown up a lot in two days. He is not a child any more," she said.

"Lizzie, you really are amazing. The idea of taking Thomas had occurred to me, but I thought it wouldn't be fair on you. We don't know much about these natives; there are so many conflicting reports. Some say the men are not to be trusted, but we can't really blame them for defending their land. I really don't know what to expect, but I am quite sure that Robert Knopwood would agree that we have a responsibility to follow Maria and at least make sure that she is accepted by her people."

"Yes, my love. Poor girl, I hope she won't be disillusioned. I can't imagine her taking off all her clothes, especially with winter coming. I hope she took her shoes."

Alice had already dropped off to sleep again and her mother was glad. Moments later she tucked her into their bed beside the hot bricks. She had food to pack in a hurry, and the medicine box to check. There was so much to think about. Perhaps a present for Dreenee and Ningermaner?

When Thomas appeared he couldn't believe his ears. His father was actually telling him to saddle up Ginger and Bess and to collect the pigeons.

"Can I really come, Papa?" he asked excitedly.

"Yes, Thomas. But the going could be rough. It's a man-sized job you are taking on and there's no time to waste. I'll get the saddlebags and blankets and the hobbles. What else do I need, Lizzie? Oh, yes! Flints and another pocket knife and whistle."

Next Edward went to the bedroom and picked up his fowling piece which he placed in its holster under his coat.

Lizzie's heart was thumping as she cut up hunks of cold meat and bread. Edward she knew would be safer with Thomas there. Maybe they would see Dreenee. But was it fair to Thomas? It was so hard for her to know what was right and wrong in this new land.

Icy puddles had turned to mud but frost lay about in the shady places; there was no time to waste. Edward glanced at the sun. They had made good time, he thought, as they trotted down the gully beside a creek, eyes to the ground.

Within half an hour they had climbed out of the next gully. Here Edward paused to scan the hills. Below them the creek joined a larger creek, and at the junction a haze of smoke hung low in a clump of wattles.

"Thomas, look! I think we may be getting closer. There's smoke ahead. Can you hear anything?"

Intently they looked and listened, but the only sounds were magpies and now and then the call of the soldier bird. While his father held both horses, Thomas walked cautiously towards the smoke of a smouldering campfire. He was about to return to his father when, to his surprise, he heard his name spoken from above. He looked up to see Dreenee swing himself out of a yellow gum and land almost at his feet!

"Thomas!" Dreenee repeated, a wide grin on his face. Then, without waiting, he bounded over to the horses. "Horse!" he exclaimed.

"Where is Maria?" Edward asked him, but Dreenee didn't seem to understand. He patted Bess, and studied her hoofprints.

"Alice?" he asked. Edward nodded and smiled, and Dreenee seemed content. Thomas wanted to help Dreenee on to Bess, but his father said "No, Thomas, not now. We must have our wits about us. Maybe there are more natives among the trees and I don't like the look of that mist. It's closing in fast. If we don't leave soon we may not find our way home."

Even as Edward spoke, an old woman appeared. There was an aura of authority about her as she looked straight into Edward's eyes and pulled Dreenee away from the horses.

Edward dismounted and all the time her eyes never left his face. He reached into the saddlebag, sensing that Ningermaner was about to move away, and there, on the other side of his horse, was Maria!

"Master," she wavered, "this is Ningermaner . . . who, with Dreenee, brought Alice home."

"Maria!" cried Edward and Thomas together. But the young woman said quietly, "No, I am Pungertenner. Master, please do not make me return with you. The farm will be attacked if you do, and I couldn't bear the thought of your family being hurt because of me."

"Your mistress and I have been most concerned about you," Edward spoke carefully. "Now I know you have found your people and wish to stay, I can ride home happily ..." Out of the corner of his eye Edward suddenly saw two more women peering from behind a large tree. As he continued to speak they crept closer, sensing all was well. "I can ride home happily," continued Edward, "and tell your mistress. You have the right to choose to go with your people. We only hope you will travel safely."

Ningermaner stood silently watching. She had put a holding spell around the rest of the band so that they couldn't turn back. She smiled and asked, "Alice?"

It was a happy group of people who stood talking about Alice. Pungertenner seemed to be proud of both parties and enjoyed acting as interpreter. Even Ningermaner soon felt more relaxed and asked several questions. Presently Edward brought out a few trinkets that Lizzie had packed. He passed Pungertenner her brush and comb and toothbrush. She showed their friends how to use them and the women laughed. They were indeed fascinating! Next came a pocket knife and Dreenee's eyes lit up. "Thank you," he said. Then Pungertenner looked at her master. "Do you have flints with you? The most useful thing you could give us would be a box of flints. Dreenee and I could teach our People how to make fire."

"A splendid idea, . . . P . . . Pungertenner," said Edward, as he gave them a little box containing a few of the precious flints.

Dreenee was beside himself with joy. He wanted to carry the box but Ningermaner intervened and put it in her pouch, so he moved over towards the pony. How he would love to be given a pony! He began stroking Bess, but Ningermaner knew what he was thinking. The People, she knew, didn't want horses. If the Intruders saw them with a horse it would only cause trouble. She was about to explain this to Dreenee when she heard a most unusual sound coming from the pouch thing on the pony. She peeped inside and saw the pigeons. Quickly Thomas rushed over and closed the saddlebag flap, but he was almost too late. Already one pigeon was on its way home.

Realising what had happened, Edward made haste to leave. He spoke briefly to Pungertenner. "Will you thank Ningermaner and Dreenee? We will never be able to thank them enough. And we will never forget you, Pungertenner. Like the swallow perhaps you will come and see us, but we will never expect you to stay." Edward swung into the saddle and Thomas hugged Pungertenner. "Goodbye," he said. "Tell Dreenee to come and see us. He can ride my pony and we promise that we will never lock him up again!"

Thomas sprang into the saddle and turned to wave farewell, but they had already disappeared beyond the mist-enshrouded trees as silently as they had come.

31. The Platypus Shoes

Dreenee's head was in a whirl as his small family group followed Mannerganner. It was hard to believe that Pungertenner was travelling with them!

Sometimes he walked close to her, holding her hand, and sometimes he raced on ahead, climbing trees or throwing stones. Stone-throwing was a wonderful way of coping with that bubbling-over feeling and it was so important to be a good stone-thrower.

The men walked apart, listening as they hunted, and Dreenee noticed that they were glancing surreptitiously at Pungertenner with admiration in their eyes. The women were staring at her unashamedly and talking and laughing among themselves. Sometimes they even mimicked Pungertenner's rather clumsy way of walking, lifting imaginary skirts to step over logs and then laughing too loudly. And some of the children kept close to her, wanting to touch her strange clothes, then scampering away again with nervous giggles.

Only Ningermaner walked quietly with long dignified

strides, very much in control of the situation and ready to rebuke anyone who dared to offend. Close to Ningermaner walked Pungertenner, her eyes cast down and her bare feet feeling their unaccustomed way over the rocks and sharp sticks. Sometimes her long skirt became caught in the undergrowth and she stumbled. Now and then her eyes would meet Dreenee's and his warm young heart would ache for the pain he saw in them.

Already, before they had walked for half a day, he could tell that her feet were sore. He considered turning back to the place where she had hidden her shoes, but even as he thought about it he knew that he could not get there and back before they made camp for the night. Instead he climbed up into the arms of an old gum tree, for he needed time to think. Somehow something must be done before Pungertenner's feet became really sore.

He could see from his tree a river not far ahead. Sun was now walking across the top of Sky so Mannerganner, he thought, was almost sure to call a halt there. He emptied his head of worry and sent a 'help' message out to his magpies.

"Come on, magpies. You are the clever ones. How can we help Pungertenner?" he asked in an urgent undertone, willing them to catch his plea.

It was a long walk to the Seafood Land and Dreenee was tormented with the fear that Pungertenner might be left behind. He had studied shoes at the settlement. They were very complicated things and made no sense to him at all, but it was obvious that Pungertenner needed shoes now. Perhaps he could make some sort of foot-covering for her out of bark or skins?

So preoccupied was Dreenee that he did not hear his magpies until he felt one fluttering down to settle next to him in the tree. It was the wise old leader. Soon others arrived. They looked intently at him, warbling softly as they let their plan flow into his head. Then they flew noisily down towards the river. So loud was their happy Travel Song that Dreenee was sure the People would stop and stare, but only one person followed them with her eyes. It was Ningermaner. No-one else appeared to notice — the bush was alive with birds.

Dreenee swung lightly down from the tree. He went straight to Ningermaner.

"Can I carry your rush basket?" he asked. She knew what he was thinking; their thoughts flowed in the silent sharing of a secret.

Clasping the basket firmly, Dreenee followed his birds down to the river. Presently they came to a glade where treeferns and blackwoods grew, and here in a quiet shady backwater of the river the magpies settled down on the bank. Immediately in front of him was a platypus burrow! He could see the web-footed tracks which led into the burrow and did not come out, and he smiled gleefully at the magpies. The platypus, he knew, would be resting while Sun climbed across the top of Sky. Never before had he hunted one, but he knew that they always built their burrows in the late summer when the river was low. It was a clever custom, for when the river swelled with rain one entrance would be under water and the soft eggs and babies would be safe from preying animals. Selecting a stout digging stick, the boy began to dig.

The mud was soft around the burrow and Dreenee marvelled about the clever ways of these quaint creatures as he dug deeper and deeper, following the passage into the bank. At last he came upon them. Both were big and the male had a sharp spur on each hind leg. The boy knew he must be careful, because the spur was poisonous.

There was no time to waste. Already they were angry and afraid, and therefore dangerous. With quick blows Dreenee killed the two animals. Then, taking a sharp stone scraper from Ningermaner's rush basket, he skinned the warm bodies. It was the first time he had skinned this animal, and when at last he had peeled away the thick strong skin he was very pleased with himself.

He splashed and rolled in the cool waters, grinning at his magpies, but much to his surprise they flew away, and he knew he must follow them. In next to no time he was racing after them with two thick skins and the basket in one hand, and in the other one the two limp bodies of meat carried upside down by four little webbed feet.

Dreenee's family band was resting under some overhanging stringybarks beside a creek when he reached them. The men were a little apart from the others and the women and children were busy around a small fire, but there was no sign of Ningermaner or Pungertenner.

Looking about him, he soon saw the soft curling smoke of another fire a little way off. Here he found Pungertenner cooling her feet in the running water while Ningermaner rubbed a thick layer of grease and ashes over her body. On the fire, tongues of orange flame were licking at her discarded clothes.

Dreenee was fascinated! He stood watching as the red skirt and blouse crumbled and faded until they were no more than a handful of grey ashes. Then he walked over to help his grandmother smear Pungertenner's skin. However, much to his surprise, as soon as he touched her the young girl hid her face behind her long hair and began to sob.

Dreenee was at a loss to know what to do. He could not understand why she cried. Perhaps his hands were too rough? Her skin certainly felt very soft, not greasy and firm like his mother's; and she had some very nasty scratches on her legs.

Very gently he rubbed more soft fat on her back, but Pungertenner only cried more loudly and ran away behind a bush, clutching a skin cloak to her breasts. Dreenee's troubled eyes met Ningermaner's. He was close to tears. Through his confusion he heard Ningermaner talking to him.

"We must give Pungertenner time to re-learn the ways of the People. She has lived too long with white people and has been taught strange customs. She has been taught that her body must be hidden behind clothes. Shame still clings to her like a cold clammy cloak. Wait here and I will go to her with another skin."

Alone by the fire Dreenee pondered. How could it be wrong to be naked? None of Droemerdeene's People hid their bodies behind clothes. What was there to hide? A body was either young or old or in-between, and it was either male or female . . . White people certainly had some clever ideas like flints for making fire and pots for cooking food, but Dreenee was quite sure that wearing clothes was not clever. Apart from shame, clothes could be seen from a great distance. Now that Pungertenner's clothes had been burnt they would all be safer, he decided.

Pensively the young boy spread the two platypus skins out to dry by the fire. Then he selected two oval stones from the river and put them on the hot coals. When the stones were hot, he stretched a skin over each one, keeping the fur on the inside, and shaped it like a foot.

When Ningermaner emerged from the tea-tree thicket with Pungertenner a few paces behind her, Dreenee did not look up. Soon Ningermaner was squatting down beside him, with admiration shining in her eyes as she studied the skins, and out of the corner of his eye he could see Pungertenner moving closer. He could see her feet and the nasty scratches on her legs, but he kept his eyes on Ningermaner as together they stretched the skins and dried them on the hot stones.

Whatever Pungertenner's shame was, he must not grieve her by looking at her body. He couldn't bear to make her cry again. Instead he carefully placed the platypus meat on the ashes, turning it over as it roasted, all the while thinking about shoes. Surely shoes could not also be something to do with this shame? No-one could possibly want to hide feet in shoes. Toes were very useful. They could tell things like wet and dry, hot and cold, smooth and rough, but trapped inside shoes toes would be useless for gripping and would become soft. Everyone at the white man's house wore shoes, he remembered. They probably never ever walked about in the bush without them!

The smell of cooking meat made Pungertenner very hungry. She had not eaten all day. She moved closer to the fire, not knowing if it were hunger for the meat which drew her most, or a longing to become one of the People. She squatted down near Ningermaner, grateful for the skin which the old woman had tied around her waist like an apron, and the other one which covered her shoulders and her breasts. She peeped about, curious to know more about the platypus skins. Dreenee, looking straight into her eyes and grinning broadly said:

"Shoes for Pungertenner!"

Admiration for Dreenee shone in her face, easing her shame and the pain in her sore feet. Presently she was stretching one foot forward and watching as Ningermaner and Dreenee fitted a skin and made small holes in it, using a sharp pointed bone from a platypus leg. Then Ningermaner produced some kangaroo sinews from her basket. These were just right for lacing, and she began to sew the skin. It was much more difficult than she had thought. None of the People sewed skins together — until now there had been no need. Dreenee, who was turning the meat, saw the problem. The holes were not big enough. He squatted down next to his grandmother and made each hole bigger. Then he threaded the sinew through the bigger holes, very slowly and rather clumsily. He felt rather proud. It was nice to be more clever than Ningermaner sometimes. He smiled to himself, then quickly tried to hide it, not wanting to hurt his grandmother's feelings. After all he had seen Alice's mother sewing; he had an unfair advantage.

So intent were the couple as they made the first shoe that they had forgotten about Pungertenner. Very soon her nimble fingers had the other skin made into a shoe and when they looked again she was fitting it on her foot!

"Pungertenner! How clever you are!" Ningermaner said, scarcely believing her own eyes as she and Dreenee admired the neatly fitted foot-covering.

Soon they were all laughing together and Pungertenner's eyes were shining. It was simply wonderful to hear her own name being used instead of that hateful name 'Maria' which she had heard for so many years. Already her clothes and some of the other ways of the settlers belonged to the past. She was Pungertenner again and she did not feel clumsy or useless. She could sew better than Ningermaner or Dreenee; this was a good beginning. Probably there would be many more things which she could teach her People.

The young woman's face was radiant as she helped them finish the other shoe and fit it on her foot.

32. The Old Ways

The laughter and the smell of cooking meat aroused the attention of three women and a crowd of children. Soon they were peering through the tea-trees, and when they saw the foot coverings on the strange young woman's feet they were overcome with curiosity. Suddenly they were crowding around, wanting to feel them and try them on. Pungertenner was the centre of attention, and she soon realised that no-one was staring at her body — they stared only at her shoes!

Almost overcome with joy, Pungertenner devoured the meat which Ningermaner passed to her. Copying the others, half reclined on one elbow, she shared morsels with the little children. It was nice to eat with her fingers again and she enjoyed licking them afterwards like everyone else. Most of all she simply loved being called Pungertenner!

As they ate, Ningermaner gave her the names of the three young women and all the little children. The three women were from Ningermaner's family — her daughters Longameena and Moonah, and her daughter-in-law Manganinnie. They all greeted her and told her their husbands often ate around a separate fire, as they were then.

It was wonderful to see so many happy little children, but hard to hold so many names in her head. Some of them were curious about her hair and the two skins she wore, and every one of them wanted to feel her strange foot-coverings and to say her name. They would race away to splash in the river and come rushing back again to have yet another look at her, while their mothers smiled fondly.

Pungertenner, watching them, again longed for her own little children with big brown eyes and lots of tight woolly curls. Pensively her hand went to her own head of long, tightly coiled locks and she suddenly regretted that it was not cropped short like those of Ningermaner and the other women. Shyly she touched Longameena's head, feeling the short tight curls.

"Hair," she said, giving them the white man's word. "Pungertenner same as Longameena, Manganinnie, Moonah. Not same as man."

What a happy laughing time it was as two women collected sharp stone scrapers from their rush baskets, eager to help shave Pungertenner's head. Dreenee was all smiles as he watched the long black locks fall away. He watched as Ningermaner powdered some charcoal and lovingly dusted it over Pungertenner's face; and he watched as Manganinnie smeared red ochre over her forehead and chin. Every moment Pungertenner was looking more like one of the People.

All the little children gathered round, silently watching this strange woman who looked more and more like the others. They snatched up the long, twisted curls as they were cut from her head and smelt and felt them. Pungertenner smiled at them with the gentlest smile Ningermaner and her family had ever seen. Everyone was smiling and Dreenee was almost bursting with happiness, for he knew his mother and all his aunts liked Pungertenner.

Of course there would be many more men and women in the camp soon, as new family groups joined them for the long journey to the Seafood Land. Ningermaner and the others were careful to show no sign of their concern that Pungertenner had no tribal markings, but Dreenee knew she would be stared at by others of the tribe, as they arrived.

Even as he thought these things Dreenee could see two

young men peeping surreptitiously through the bushes, overcome with curiosity. Alarmed, he glanced quickly at Ningermaner, only to know that she had already seen them. Her eyes were as fierce and proud as those of the wedge-tailed eagle as she rose to her feet and, boldly shaking her fist, pointed them out of the women's camp.

Presently the women led Pungertenner down to the river to study her new reflection, so Dreenee gathered up every lock of Pungertenner's hair that had been left scattered about and hid the footprints made by the platypus shoes. Ningermaner's eyes were smiling as her grandson stuffed the locks of Pungertenner's hair into her basket.

"Well done, Dreenee," she said. "Tonight I shall plait you a cord from Pungertenner's hair to wear around your neck. It will bring you good luck."

The youngster beamed. To have his own cord! And made from Pungertenner's hair! He felt almost grown-up, for such cords usually adorned only the young men.

One glance at Pungertenner told Dreenee that she had been pleased with her new reflection, but he also knew that she was still very shy. He moved closer to her, for he could see Mannerganner wading the river, and behind him a noisy horde of People. All his aunts and Ningermaner gathered around Pungertenner, for they too sensed that the next few minutes would not be easy for her.

In single file the men followed Mannerganner through the water, each one taking a furtive look at Pungertenner, and trying not to show surprise or amusement, while the beautiful young woman hung her head and played nervously with her long blue-green necklace. The women and children stared openly. Some of them laughed; others pointed at the strange woman, instantly rousing the anger of Ningermaner and her family. They brandished sticks in the air and hurled stones at the offenders, shouting abuse until the long line had moved past them.

Dreenee was delighted to see such loyalty shown to Pungertenner, but her gentle ways both confused and worried him.

"Ningermaner," he asked, "why did Pungertenner not fight back?"

"Living with the Intruders has taken all her fight away. She has probably been stared at many times by the white people, simply because she is black, and no doubt she has been beaten or punished in some other way for even raising her voice in anger. Pungertenner has much to forget, and much to learn, and many things to teach us when she is used to us. She now needs lots of love, and to feel that she belongs with us."

After Ningermaner had spoken Dreenee went over to Pungertenner, with a great big smile on his face. He affectionately hugged her, and much to his surprise she kissed him lightly on the lips.

Everyone was amazed! Surely this must be another custom that Pungertenner had learnt from the white ones?

Confused, Dreenee took Pungertenner's hand and led her along the track, not letting his smile show. Ningermaner walked close to Pungertenner with silent purposeful strides, while her daughters and daughter-in-law followed, thinking mostly about kissing, but saying nothing. Close behind them their children frolicked about, throwing stones and laughing.

Instead of spreading out and hunting as they went along as was the custom, the men fell into small groups to talk about Pungertenner and her strange foot-coverings, and her two kangaroo skins. They had of course seen foot-coverings made from bull kelp when someone had injured a foot on sharp rocks by the sea, but nothing quite like Pungertenner's. These were definitely made from skins, but with the fur side in, it was difficult to decide which animal the skins had come from. And the very thought of a young woman wearing two more skins about her body, on such a warm day, brought a twinkle of amusement to every man's face. An old woman might wear a second skin around her waist when there was a heavy fall of snow, but Pungertenner must have grown soft like a white woman! They all agreed that she was very beautiful, but clumsy on her feet, and extraordinarily shy.

The journey ahead would be filled with all sorts of jokes and arguments as other groups joined them on the way to the Seafood Festival. They were quite sure she would not know how to fight back if she were mocked or mimicked, but at the same time they knew that Ningermaner would stand no nonsense.

The gullies echoed with the laughter of the young men as they walked. Tomorrow Mannerganner would lead them to the Lake of Shallow Waters, where they would camp for a few days while their smoke called the other bands together.

33. *Mannerganner*

Mannerganner was sullen as he moved away carrying his spears. Ningermaner had no right to make plans for this strange woman who did not belong to their Big River tribe. She had arranged it all behind his back. Even if Pungertenner's own tribe did not attack them, her white master might yet follow her and the safety of his People was threatened enough without this added risk.

His eyes were fierce, but behind them confusion mingled with fear so he walked fast, his head held high. He laughed aloud for reassurance, but it was a thin laugh which rippled on the brink of anger, brittle as the dry twigs and bark which snapped beneath his feet; and it faded into emptiness leaving behind only confusion and a bleak sense of despair.

"Was he not Leader?" he asked aloud. "Had he not been chosen by the councillors to lead the Big River People on their food-gathering migrations, after Sea had so suddenly taken away his wonderful old teacher, Ningermaner's husband?"

Because of Sea there had been no funeral pyre, and no bones or ashes to wear. Sea gave to Mannerganner only the memory of the huge wave, and an empty place in his heart for his old friend. Being angry with Sea helped, but it was still a lonely place as a leader.

Ningermaner's fierce old eyes seemed always to look right inside him, and sometimes it seemed to him that she even put ideas into his head and words into his mouth! She made him feel restless and unsure of himself. She was fast becoming a law unto herself, and something must be done about it.

Mannerganner pondered over the situation as he led his People. He could of course call up his help-spirits and try to point her out of his band. She had sons and daughters and many grandchildren in other family groups who would welcome her, but unfortunately she had formed a strong attachment to Moonah's man-child Dreenee. He knew she would not stay away for long.

In his despair, evil thoughts took control of Mannerganner's mind. He could wish Ningermaner evil until her body faded away and she died — but even as the thought drifted into his consciousness he pushed it aside. Had he not loved Ningermaner when he was a little child? Had she not taught him much Common Knowledge and sometimes even carried him on her back?

Mannerganner felt sorry for himself. His chosen bride had been stolen by a sealer before she was of age to wed him. She had been his childhood playmate each time he visited the Seafood Land, and the marriage had been arranged according to custom. He was only one of many men who had lost their women, but it was cold comfort. He needed his own woman, but had no authority to choose his own bride. He must await the decision of the old men.

Manfully the young Leader straightened his shoulders. He had no right to indulge in self-pity; he was shirking his responsibility to his People.

Ahead there could be stockmen or bushrangers lying in ambush, waiting to kill them or steal their women and children. Instead of dwelling on his own loneliness he should be keeping a keen lookabout. He stamped his feet hard, calling his help-spirits to walk with them and hide their tracks, and very soon he could feel them leading him away from the ancient pathway and along a creek of running water and over boulder-strewn ridges too barren to hold the message of their journey.

Looking back he could see his small band following him, trusting in his leadership, and the cloak of depression fell from his shoulders. Suddenly it was an autumn-gold day, fading into winter, and he was Mannerganner leading his People safely on the longest migration of the food-gathering cycle, over to the Seafood Land.

Pensively he spoke to his wise old friend and teacher. It was only a whisper for he was not at all sure if he had enough magic power to call him up.

"O wise Old One, my teacher, please make me stronger so that I may be worthy of your faith in me. Surely from your campfire you must know the dangers which surround us and the dangers which lie ahead. Guide us on our journey and protect us from the evil spirit."

Mannerganner paused, and then he asked very quietly if perhaps someone around the campfires in the sky might choose for him a woman of his own. Overhead a rainbow appeared and from the rainbow Mannerganner heard the voice of his old teacher, who was Ningermaner's husband. "We are watching over you. Even now we give to you many more help-spirits, and very soon you will be able to hide in your own shadow and keep other people out of your thoughts. You will become a great Leader, your own woman will walk with you, and you will not be lonely any more."

Mannerganner listened in wonder, for never before had he been given his own private message. As the rainbow faded, a love-song swelled in his heart and overflowed, warmer than sunlight, filling the gully with rich melodious overtones of song.

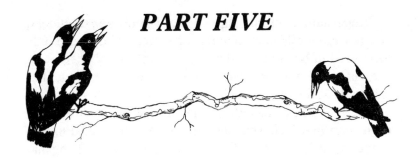

PART FIVE

34. The Lake of Shallow Waters

The Lake of Shallow Waters shone warm and welcoming as Mannerganner led his People over the last gentle slope. Reeds danced in the light breeze, glittering gold and brown and soft, soft green. Overhead birds swooped and hovered. Skeins of mist hung low over the distant shore, and here and there the smoke of several campfires curled and drifted in the gentle sunlight.

It was good to come again to the Shallow Waters and to see the smoke of many fires. With a long drawn out guttural screech, Mannerganner made the Big River tribal call of the black cockatoo. Three times he called, and then across the shallow waters came the answering calls of several families.

Pungertenner splashed and paddled about in the shallow waters. Her legs ached from the long walk, and her feet felt hot and swollen. Watching Manganinnie dive and swim, she felt foolish as she hugged her two skins close to her. She had not been in the water like that for a long time; it did look fun, and no-one was looking . . .

She was about to slide unnoticed into the water when Dreenee and some of his young friends came rushing down to the water's edge. Proudly he showed the children the platypus shoes, neatly placed on a log beside Pungertenner, and everyone wanted to try them on. The laughter of the children echoed across the still waters as they crowded around and played balancing games on the huge fallen log, taking turns to wear the new shoes.

Pungertenner timidly slipped the skin off her shoulders, but not one child took a scrap of notice. They were only interested in her soft swollen feet and the angry blisters, so presently the young woman untied the skin around her waist and slid naked into the water.

The freedom of nakedness and the cluster of little children who had followed her into the water filled Pungertenner with joy. Seeing Dreenee's little brother, Pengana, ankle-deep in water — afraid to go further — she waded back and picked him up, hugging him tightly to her body and sang to him. Soon tears filled her eyes and overflowed into the lake; she was so happy.

Dreenee, seeing how happy Pungertenner was, swam off by himself. He didn't want her to see the joy which was spreading across his face. He had used the little children to help Pungertenner lose her shame, and it had worked! Lying along a floating log he watched them. Then, looking across to the trees all along the shore, he saw Ningermaner. She was obviously studying the trees for signs of possums; but he knew that she was also watching Pungertenner. She had been peeping inside his head and knew of his plan, and had seen how it had succeeded.

A loud "Wah! Wah!" coming from the top of a peppermint tree startled Pungertenner. All the children yelled and raced out of the water over to the tree. Dreenee scrambled up beside Pungertenner on her log and together they watched the other children crowding around the tree. High above them Moonah was working her way along a spreading bough, and almost within her reach was a spitting furry possum with its bushy tail firmly wound around the bough. A moment later Moonah grabbed it and threw it down. There was a flurry of children as they scrambled to catch the stunned animal.

All her childhood memories of the excitement of a possum hunt returned to Pungertenner as she watched Moonah swing gracefully down the tree, helped by her climbing rope. She felt clumsy and useless as she watched Moonah's strong toes seek and find each foothold. She would need to start right from the beginning with balance lessons before she could hope to climb like that.

Dreenee sensed the young woman's dejection. Simply by sitting beside her he could know what she was thinking. He must take her thoughts away. Excitedly he pointed across the water to a shallow pool surrounded by reeds. As Pungertenner watched, two big black swans glided down and settled on the water. She could hear them trumpeting as they swam about, feeding close together; and she could see Manganinnie watching them from behind a mound of dead reeds.

Presently the birds settled down to doze in the sun, and then Manganinnie slid very quietly into the water, keeping below the surface and swimming so smoothly that not a ripple was to be seen. Suddenly one bird flapped violently and disappeared beneath the surface. Startled, the other bird flew away.

Moments later they saw Manganinnie wading through the reeds dragging a large drowned swan behind her, and Dreenee, seeing the mate wheeling overhead, raced across to Manganinnie, knowing she would need help. As Pungertenner watched, the swan swooped lower, beating the air with angry black and white wings, his red beak poised and ready to attack the human who had taken away his mate. But Dreenee reached Manganinnie just in time, and thrashed at the swan with a heavy stick, driving it away.

From her log Pungertenner watched Dreenee drag the swan back to the camp, and then saw Manganinnie slip away through the reeds to look for other swans and ducks. Even as she watched, she could hear Moonah call again from another tree, and she could also see a party of men racing through the timber with their spears held high, and several kangaroos bounding ahead of them.

Men were yelling, children were rushing to join in the excitement, and overhead the sky was noisy with swans and ducks. Only Pengana lay still, sleeping contentedly as Pungertenner stroked the chubby little toes and held him close, talking softly to him:

"It doesn't really matter if I can't climb for possums like your mother, or swim underwater like Manganinnie, does it, Pengana? I care for you while they go hunting; and I need time to sort through all the things I know about the white people and their new animals, because I have more knowledge about them than anyone else here."

Pengana slumbered on, but it didn't matter. It was good to talk again in her native tongue, though presently she broke into English; this was, after all, the language she spoke freely.

"Did you know I lived on a farm, Pengana? I had to work for a family of white people and sleep in their house until Dreenee and his magpies helped me to escape. Now here I am! Back with my own People! It's so exciting — but I do feel very shy. Not many of the Big River tribe can understand my dialect. Even Ningermaner can't understand all my words, because I belong to another tribe, and what is worse, I have no tribal markings. I know everyone is trying not to notice, but I do feel embarrassed. And I feel embarrassed too, without any clothes, because for years I've been dressed up like a white girl and taught that it's wicked to walk about naked.

"The white ones have lots of good ideas, which I must share with the People, but I'm sure that wearing clothes isn't one of them. Oh, Pengana! You have no idea the amount of work that clothes make! The time spent making them and mending them! And washing and ironing them! I never want to see a wash-tub, or a clothes line, or a flat-iron again.

"And as for living in one place! It makes so much work living in a house, sweeping and dusting; scrubbing and polishing. Even meals are cooked in pots, and served on dishes, and eaten at a table, and then of course things have to be washed up afterwards. The hours I have spent working over hot fires and sinks of water! I don't want to see another pile of dirty dishes for as long as I live!"

Pungertenner paused and looked about. There was no-one near enough to hear, except Pengana, and he was still dozing peacefully. She had enjoyed herself talking aloud; it helped her to sort out what was valuable information to share with the People and what was not. Certainly houses and clothes and possessions were not good ideas. However, the white people's language and hunting and travelling habits and their tracks were important, and so were their new animals, because every day more settlers were spreading out over the Land of her People.

Pensively the young woman stroked Pengana's chubby little legs, and he woke and smiled up at her.

"Would you like me to tell you about all the new animals?" she said. "I'll start with Horse, because he's my favourite. Horses are very important to the newcomers because they can travel fast, and the white people always seem to be in such a hurry! Sometimes they sit on Horse's back and sometimes Horse pulls them along while they sit in a cart. Carts come in all sizes and shapes, and so do horses for that matter. And you probably won't believe me, but I have ridden on Horse and been pulled along by him in all sorts of carts. I even know the size by the tracks they leave behind."

Pengana gazed at her with such a quaint expression that Pungertenner laughed. "So you don't believe me, eh? Well, it's true. I'm a good rider. It's a wonderful feeling being high up and travelling sometimes faster than the biggest kangaroo. Dreenee had a ride on Horse when he was captured and was brought back to the farm, so if you don't believe me, ask Dreenee".

So intent was Pungertenner that she was quite unaware that Lugga and Dreenee had crept up behind the log where she was sitting. For some time they had silently stood listening in fascination to the strange language, but when Dreenee heard the white man's word 'horse' and his own name, he could hold his silence no longer.

"Horse!" he yelled, bounding forward, his mind bubbling over with questions about Horse. But already Lugga was speaking to Pungertenner: "I've seen a small horse", he said. "I followed its tracks after Alice had fallen off it. I found it caught up by the trailing rope-thing on a stump . . ."

His words faded away for he realised that Pungertenner wasn't even listening. Instead she was groping around in the shallow water. Moments later she had several flat wet stones beside her on the log, and on one stone she was scratching the outline of Horse with a pointed flint.

Lugga could scarcely believe his eyes. His People never drew animals like this! Hand stencils, yes, and lines and circles; but nothing as complicated as a four-legged animal. "Horse!" he exclaimed, and even as he spoke Pungertenner drew a boy on the horse's back.

"Lugga on Horse?" she said very slowly, handing him the work of art. Lugga was lost for words while he fondled his new treasure, then he passed another stone to Pungertenner.

"Dreenee on Horse?" he said, and while the boys waited Pungertenner drew another horse and rider. "Dreenee on Horse", she said.

The youngsters wanted to race away and show the drawings to everyone, but Pungertenner needed more time. "No", she said, "time later." These words Dreenee understood, so he placed the two stones carefully back in the shallow water beside Pungertenner's sore feet and waded away through the reeds to find a quiet place to think, for he had remembered the animal picture books at the farm. He should have shared this Common Knowledge with Lugga and his friends long ago.

He called to Lugga, and soon they were trying their skills at drawing the outline of Horse, and discussing the possibilities of drawing. When Pungertenner was ready, perhaps she would teach them many things even without the use of words, they decided.

35. The Songwoman

Pungertenner was deep in thought as she sat on the log
cooling her swollen feet after Dreenee and Lugga had
scampered away. It was the first time in two days that she
had had time to think. Her mind raced on and excitement
glowed in her lovely brown eyes at the thought of seeing the
tribal lands of her childhood again and finding her family.
Perhaps even the husband who had been chosen by her
parents would still be waiting for her and then soon she
would have babies of her very own!

Yet even as her thoughts reached out in hope, the pain in
her feet brought her swiftly back to reality. How could she
walk such a long way on her useless, throbbing feet? Even
wearing Dreenee's platypus boots, long distance walking
would be almost impossible. If Manilerganner called on the
People to move again she would soon be left behind. A cold
fear washed over her, taking away the warmth of Sun.

Pensively the young woman studied each foot, hating the
stiffly curled toes which had been crushed into shoes. They
were soft and weak and ugly — and they were very sore.
Angry blisters covered the soles of both feet and her legs
were scratched and bleeding. She returned them to the cool
muddy water and tried to forget them.

Cuddling Pengana to her, she thought again about her
parents, and her eyes became deep pools of misery as she
realised how many seasons had come and gone since she
had been stolen from them. They too might have been
kidnapped or killed and the same thing could happen to her
if she had to remain behind. A bushranger or woodcutter
might find her, or perhaps a stock-keeper, and then she
would never reach the Seafood Land and find her family.

Ningermaner was turning the meat on her fire when she
felt the first twitch in her shoulder and immediately she
looked to the place where Pungertenner was cooling her
feet. How grey were the gloomy thoughts which surrounded the young woman! Something was wrong.

Ningermaner listened intently to her help-spirits and

then she waded out to the log. On a flat piece of bark she carried a mixture of oil from the blue-tongued lizard and ashes from the fire. Softly she crooned the magic healing song as she smeared the paste on Pungertenner's sore feet, and as she sang, the thick grey air lifted and drifted away, leaving in its place a soft pink light.

Together they sat, side by side on the huge old log, watching the colours grow and spread around them, and gazing at their own reflections in the water: the old one and the young one, and the sleeping child. Ningermaner could feel magic. Presently, as she watched, their reflections faded and she could see the face of her husband. For one long moment their eyes met, and then he turned to Pungertenner and spoke:

Greetings, Pungertenner. I come to you from our campfires in the River of Stars to tell you that you have nothing to fear. We send healing for your feet through Ningermaner's hands, and we put a holding spell around Mannerganner. He will camp here until your feet are healed, for the water-birds are plentiful.

Look into my eyes and presently you will see again the nature spirits you knew so well as a little child. Listen to them, and very soon they will give to you your first song, for we name you Pungertenner the Songwoman.

Slowly the gentle face of the Old One faded and Pungertenner watched in fascination as tiny water spirits came to twinkle and dance around her feet. Soon they were singing. She began to feel the words of their song tremble at the back of her throat and her innermost being thrilled to their rhythm.

Mannerganner was returning to camp when he felt the Land tremble beneath his feet. The air had become so still that not one leaf fell as he led his hunters through the trees, and when they came in sight of the Lake of Shallow Waters they saw a brilliant pink light. Mannerganner leaned his spears against a tree and walked silently down to the water's edge and silently his hunters followed him. Soon the women and children joined him on the shore.

Dreenee had been collecting swans' down and wattle gum to line Pungertenner's shoes when his whole body began to tremble and he could feel the Old Ones very near. Not one ripple drifted across the surface of the lake and Wind was still, yet a pink glow was rising and spreading out around the place where Pungertenner sat. Then, as he watched, he could see Ningermaner wading ashore with Pengana on her back.

He opened his inside eye and peeped into the pink circle of light, and there he saw the water spirits and the radiant smile on Pungertenner's face. Her lips were trembling! He scrambled up into the strong spreading arms of an old stringybark tree, for he wanted to be alone. His magpies soon fluttered down softly into the higher branches.

A hush fell over the Land, and then Pungertenner burst into song. The clear ringing words spread out across the lake and climbed the hills, coming again and again, the low tone rising to a higher key in expressive harmony.

Mannerganner stood motionless as Pungertenner gave the song of Dreenee the Magpie Boy to the People. He knew instinctively that this was a Given Song, and that he must soak up the words and store them in his mind, for tonight when Moon was ready it must be sung exactly as given. This was the Law.

Three times the song was given, and as the last notes faded away Mannerganner moved forward alone, and waded out to greet the new Songwoman.

"It is my great privilege to welcome you as Songwoman", he said; and then there was a long pause. He became lost for words under the spell of her beauty. As his eyes looked into her soft brown ones he thought illogically of the shy little possum-mouse, and he suddenly wanted only to pick her up and carry her gently away to his own lonely campfire. When he next spoke his voice was expressionless.

"You have given to us a very beautiful song. Tonight when Moon is ready I will give it to the People." Turning away he began to wade ashore, but he hesitated and turned and then, perhaps because of her sore feet, picked up Pungertenner gently in his arms. As he put her down on the shore she did not feel the pain in her feet and she did not feel shame. She had completely forgotten about her two kangaroo skins on the log beside her platypus shoes. She could feel only the gentle arms of Mannerganner, and his thoughts flowing into her mind as he wordlessly walked away. It was a strange new feeling which brought the colour to her cheeks, so she hung her head and fondled the tiny warrener shells which Ningermaner had so recently given her.

Peeping through her long black lashes, Pungertenner stood motionless watching Mannerganner as he disappeared along the shoreline. Moments later the women and children were flocking round her, welcoming her to the tribe and beseeching her to sing again; but the nearness of Mannerganner still clung to her and she wanted only to be alone. Sensing Pungertenner's urgent need, Ningermaner called the families back to their tasks of preparing the evening meal and adorning their bodies ready for the festival.

36. The Brink of Time

Dreenee was glad of the strength of the old tree, for he had seen and heard everything which had taken place within the magic circle of pink light. His spirit-person had shared the vision of the Old Ones and, when the Song of the Magpie Boy was given, a new understanding had come to him. No longer were the warblings of the magpies a muffled message. He could now ask them anything about the whereabouts of his tribesmen or the Intruders and their strange animals, and the magpies would supply him with that information. Even now he was aware of the new energy which flowed from the magpies, and as they warbled softly in the branches above him he felt his innermost being fuse with every feature of the Land, until a bond of kinship with all of creation encompassed him. So powerful was the sensation his whole body shuddered with a new twinge of manhood which both bewildered and excited him. Pondering over the New Knowledge which had come to him through the Given Song, he knew that his childhood days would fade with the setting sun; and with the dawn of another day he would know many changes and his life would take on a new meaning.

In the distance Dreenee could see Pungertenner turn and walk back along the shore. Closing his mind to everything about him, he soaked up every thought which flickered through her mind and knew she had left behind her the ways of the white ones. She was indeed Pungertenner of the People, ready to walk through all her tomorrows beside Mannerganner.

Concentrating hard, Dreenee willed his spirit-person to go forward into the future and presently he could see Pungertenner with stars in her eyes, as Mannerganner led her away from the Festival of Spring to their own private campsite beside the River of Singing Waters.

Dreenee was beside himself with joy. Not only was Pungertenner accepted into the tribe and chosen by the Old Ones to be their Songwoman but when Spring came she would be given to Mannerganner by the older men of the Big River tribe. It was too wonderful for words!

The young boy wanted to leap down from the tree and rush to her side, telling her all he knew, but the wiser one in him sat on, softly warbling with the magpies while he collected his own thoughts together. As the last notes faded Dreenee looked to the log where Pungertenner had so recently been sitting. The two *larner* skins and the shoes he had made from *oonah* were all that remained. Pungertenner it seemed had already left her shame behind on the log and even though he couldn't quite understand white man's concept of shame, Dreenee was delighted, for soon the kangaroo skins and the platypus shoes would be lost in the shadows of Night. Maybe a night owl would snatch them away, or a prowling scavenger devour them, but it didn't really matter. They were no longer needed. One day he would make up a song and dance about Pungertenner and her two skins! How everyone would laugh! Even the story of her platypus shoes would be good entertainment.

Pensively Dreenee thought about all the things he and his magpies had tried to share with the People: the possessions from the white man's settlement, goat's milk, the booming magic firestick called musket, the ticking pocket-watch called Time, the useful round pot he kept at the bottom of the river. The People might never be ready for these things, he realised. However they had accepted the greatest gift of them all, Pungertenner. And very soon she would be sharing with everyone the wonders of the white man's fire flints.

Watching Pungertenner paddle along the shore, coming closer to the camp of the women, he chuckled to himself. Even Pungertenner of the gentle ways could be angry if she realised he had not only studied her thoughts, but even peeped into her future! And as for Mannerganner, Dreenee was certain he would be furious if he found out that a mere boy had been prying into his private affairs and had a gift greater than his own. Laughing aloud and feeling very pleased with himself, Dreenee burst into magpie song. Moments later the magpies were singing with him and he could understand every word. It was a Given Song which told of Pungertenner and the joys of motherhood.

Sun continued the journey of day as Pungertenner came close to the camp of the women. Pausing, she looked across the silver soft waters as they sparkled in the late afternoon sun and beyond the lake to the mountains climbing to meet the sky. How strong they were! Many things would change, she knew, but the mountains would remain unchanging and timeless as the seas which surrounded the Land of Southern Star.

Aware that she was being watched, not only by the

women and children but by someone else, Pungertenner's eyes were drawn to the tree where Dreenee waited, and waves of gratitude went out to him. But for Dreenee, she would still be washing pots and pans instead of soaking up the wonders of the world about her. Later she would seek him out and tie around his neck her locks of hair which Ningermaner had so skilfully woven for him; but now she must go to Ningermaner, for Sun was walking down towards the hills and Sun would not wait for anyone.

Her head held high and a gentle smile upon her face, Pungertenner walked into camp. The warmth of the women and children as they flocked about her with words of welcome filled her with a glorious feeling of belonging she had never known before. All the pent-up emotions of the last few days came to the surface, and she hung her head and wept. Through her tears she could see Ningermaner move to her side. While the women watched, Ningermaner placed the small pouch containing the precious flints around her neck and began to chant a warmth into it which would bring wisdom to Mannerganner's lips and comfort to the People; and the women, not knowing what was in the pouch, felt the warmth from the gift and were filled with curiosity. Fondling the little pouch, Pungertenner found comfort — and spoke:

"When can we share Fire with the People, Ningermaner?" she asked.

"We must plan it now, while the women prepare the meal," Ningermaner replied, "for later, when Moon is ready, Mannerganner will be giving us the Magpie Boy Song and he will need to know about the gift of Fire."

As Ningermaner spoke she left her mind open, wanting Dreenee to catch her words, so she wasn't surprised when he came bounding towards them.

"Go now, Dreenee, and carry our message to Mannerganner."

"What message, Ningermaner?", he asked, pretending not to know.

"You know perfectly well! I allowed my words to flow

151

into your mind. You are not as clever as you thought you were! One day your powers will be stronger than mine. But not yet!" she said with a lively twinkle in her eyes. But Dreenee could look behind her eyes, and knew she had not seen the Vision of Spring.

Laughing, Dreenee strode over to the camp of the men. He stood for a moment — straight as a tea-tree spear — then he bowed and gave his Leader the message.

"Ningermaner wishes to sit in council with you, and wants to bring Pungertenner, for they have a gift from the white man", he announced.

Mannerganner was silent for a moment while a confusion of thoughts tumbled round in his head. Firstly, only a few seasons ago, an old woman and a boy sitting in council, and now a young woman new to the tribe; and with no ceremonial markings.

"What is this gift, Dreenee?" he asked cautiously. "I must know before I let Pungertenner enter the camp of the councillors."

"It is two metal flints which white men rub together in a special way and make sparks — big enough to kindle fire", he explained.

"They make fire this way? They do not carry firesticks? Only these flints?"

"Yes, Mannerganner", Dreenee replied, enjoying himself as carrier of such news.

"Have you seen these things called flints?" Mannerganner inquired.

"Yes. I saw them at the settlement, but I wasn't allowed to touch them. Maybe we could study them and learn to make our own metal firesticks", Dreenee suggested; then rather wondered where the idea had come from. Was it the magpies putting words in his mouth? Or was it his own idea? Whichever way, it really was a good idea!

As Dreenee spoke, he became aware of the excitement swelling around him. All the councillors were silently watching Mannerganner as he pondered over Dreenee's words.

152

Then, with an air of authority, Mannerganner spoke:

"I wish for Ningermaner to come alone."

"But Mannerganner, only Pungertenner knows how to use the flints."

Mannerganner further reflected. Pungertenner had already kindled a spark in him. It seemed fitting for her to bring Fire to his People. Quickly he hid the smile which was trembling on the brink of laughter. When he spoke again his words were decisive, his eyes expressionless.

"Go then, and bring the two women with you. You also may join us."

"Oh! Thank you, Mannerganner!" Dreenee paused. "Can Lugga come too? We are the same age."

"Why not! If a young woman, new to our tribe, can sit in council with us, then it is right and proper that you and Lugga should join us. Yes, bring Lugga. Bring all the older boys."

Dreenee rushed away to the water's edge to tell Lugga. Then he hurried on, beyond the women's camp to where Ningermaner was waiting. Passing his mother, he paused and their eyes met. For one long moment he watched her nimble fingers as she mended her climbing rope, then he wended his way through the camp he knew so well: the cooking fires; the wonderful smells; babies being fed; children tumbling in play and the laughing chatter of their mothers. Taking one fleeting glance, he stored the memory of it all in his mind.

Very soon Dreenee was leading Ningermaner and Pungertenner into the men's camp, with Lugga and the older boys proudly walking behind them. When everyone was seated according to their position in the tribe, Pungertenner took the metal flints from her pouch and placed them in Mannerganner's outstretched hand.

Silently everyone waited as he turned them over and rubbed them together; then looking directly at Pungertenner he asked her to make fire.

Gracefully the young woman squatted down a few paces away and scooped together several piles of she-oak needles.

Placing her hands under the long dry leaves, she carefully rubbed the flints together and quite suddenly sparks flashed and, catching the dry leaves, flared! Pungertenner had given fire to the People! Amazement showed on every face.

"Fire! White man's fire!" they yelled; and the women, hearing them, could no longer keep away. Overpowered by their curiosity they moved closer, and the children followed them. But in the future, the younger women would always refuse to make white man's fire themselves. They would leave that to Pungertenner and the men, as they clung to the old ways of their childhood.

Only Mannerganner stood silently, feeling the flints which Pungertenner had shyly handed back to him. How warm they were! Even as he held them, adding his own warmth to that of the beautiful Songwoman's, they seemed to glow. Moments later he felt the presence of his old chief who had been Ningermaner's husband, he whose name must not be mentioned. The old chief spoke:

Greetings, Mannerganner. You did well to accept Pungertenner into your tribe. It is right also that you adopt the white man's way of making fire by friction, for there will be times in the future when you must hurry and hide and take unaccustomed pathways. Some of the old ways will no longer be suited to the changes which are to come. You must learn to bend like young trees, for your very survival will depend on your ability to change or vary your seasonal migrations; and yet pay homage to the Ancestral Beings in the age-old way.

You cannot drive the white ones away, for you do not have the numbers or the skills; and there is no other place you can go. Your roots are deep in the Mother Earth. Like trees your bodies would wither and die without these roots; your spirits are bonded to the features of the Land in such a way that the Intruders do not understand. They have no kinship with the soil, except to possess it; and you are to them like trees that stand in their way. The timeless dreaming Land can slumber no more. You stand now on the brink of time, like spears about to be hurled into a new era.

After the old chief's voice had faded, Mannerganner stood leaning against the tree trunk, his eyes drawn to the flints, his back to the excitement white man's fire had created. Fear for his People brought the moisture to his brow. How, he wondered, could the old ways change, without breaking the Dreamtime Law? Soon the People would ask many questions, but how could he answer them?

He looked about in the noisy crowd for Pungertenner, but she was nowhere to be seen. She had silently slipped away to watch the sunset.

Pungertenner was paddling her feet in the cool comforting waters when Dreenee came bounding towards her. Moments later the magpies began their glorious Sunset Song. Together they stood side by side wordlessly watching as Sun painted the Lake of Shallow Waters with ballawinne, the sacred red ochre. As the last peels of birdsong faded, a hush fell over the Land, louder than words, and in the silence Pungertenner and Dreenee knew that they were ready for the changing ways.

Taking his hands the Songwoman placed in them the braid plaited from her long locks.

"Farewell Magpie Boy", she murmured softly. "When the magpies sing I will think of you."

"Farewell Maria of the pots and pans," he replied. Pausing, Dreenee looked about, not wanting to be overheard. "Did you know", he whispered, "that tonight, when Moon is ready, Mannerganner will woo you with flowers; and you will become his chosen one?"

Pungertenner was lost for words. Her eyes soft pools of misty tears, she fondled her pouch while she collected her thoughts, wanting to ask Dreenee how he knew these things, but when she looked again he had gone.

Without a backward glance Dreenee disappeared as quickly as he had come. Sun was ready to blink and slide down behind the hills. Dreenee must adorn himself with great care, ready for the Festival. It would be for him the most important festival of his young life, for afterwards he would walk away from the women and children and camp with the men.

Tasmanian Aboriginal words

ballawinne	red ochre
draydee	wattle tree
dreenee	magpie
Droemerdeene	Ancestral Being
drogermutter	wombat
gonnanner	emu
kallerhoneyer	swan
ropettener	swan
larner	kangaroo
leehanner	blue-tongued lizard, goanna
lugga	footprint
Lynoteyer	Sea
markomemenyer	native walk
marweyanner	dolphin
menanyer	river
mitawennya	whale
naweetya	seal
Ningermaner	mother
oonah	seal
Poekenner	Rain
poorena	firestick
Raegeowropper	Evil Spirit
toebenanner	fairy penguin
tonna	fire
triggelune	ship
Trullerner	Wind
Wetar	Moon
wurrah	duck

Place names

Kutalinah	Jordan River
Leeawulena	'The Lake of Dreams' (Lake St Clair)
Loegener	'Fat Doe River' (Clyde River)
Norerucker	'River of Singing Waters' (Shannon River)
Panatana	Port Dalrymple (Launceston)
Timtumele	'The Wide River' (Derwent River)